Best Easy Day Hikes Series

Best Easy Day Hikes
Eugene, Oregon

Art Bernstein and Lynn Bernstein

FALCONGUIDES

GUILFORD, CONNECTICUT
HELENA, MONTANA

AN IMPRINT OF GLOBE PEQUOT PRESS

FALCONGUIDES®

TOPO! Explorer software and SuperQuad source maps courtesy of National Geographic Maps. For information about TOPO! Explorer, TOPO!, and Nat Geo Maps products, go to www.topo.com or www.natgeomaps.com.

Maps created by OffRoute Inc. © Morris Book Publishing, LLC

Project editor: David Legere
Layout artist: Kevin Mak

Library of Congress Cataloging-in-Publication Data is available on file.

ISBN 978-0-7627-6992-6

Printed in the United States of America

10 9 8 7 6 5 4 3 2 1

Contents

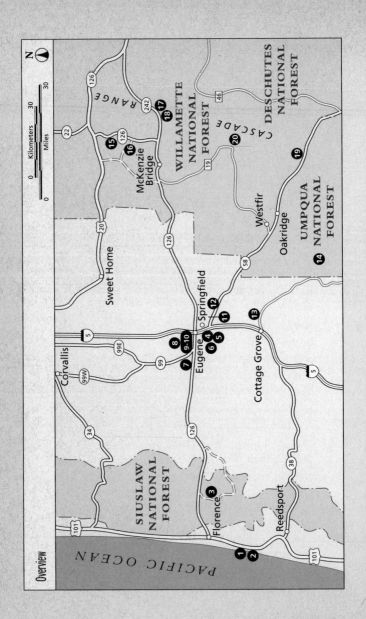

McKenzie River Area

Oakridge / Willamette Pass

Acknowledgments

The authors dedicate this book to their wonderful children, who enthusiastically encouraged their relationship, love of hiking, and commitment to this project. That includes Chris, Eric and David Pitt, Sara and Anna Bernstein, and, yes, Jennifer Bremer.

In researching this book, several individuals were extremely helpful. The authors especially thank Eric Wold at Eugene Parks and Open Space, Christy Lewis and others at the Oregon Dunes Information Center, Katura Reynolds at the Buford Park Arboretum, Mike Moskovitz at Dorris Ranch, Mykalena and others at the McKenzie River Ranger Station, and the women at the Westfir Ranger Station. We also thank David Pitt, our GPS maven, and Joanna Knower.

Introduction

The Eugene Area

This small pocket guide describes twenty of the best easy day hikes to be found within 90 miles of Eugene, Oregon. They range in length from 0.5 mile to about 4.6 miles. Eugene is Oregon's second largest city (population 153,000), and the home of the University of Oregon.

"Within 90 miles of Eugene" takes in amazingly diverse country. Lane County, of which Eugene is the county seat, is one of only two Oregon counties stretching from the Pacific Coast, over the densely forested Coast Range mountains, across the hills and farms of the Willamette Valley, and up to the rocky crest of the volcanic High Cascades Mountains, with elevations over 10,000 feet. The county includes parts of three national forests—the Siuslaw, Willamette, and Umpqua—and is one of the most trail-dense places anywhere in the US.

Every route in this book is located in Lane County, with the exception of the two McKenzie River Trail segments, which are just over the Linn County line.

Nearly everybody in Eugene hikes (or bikes or in-line skates or runs), and even inside the city limits, there are 50 miles of fantastic trails, many with a surprisingly "wilderness" feel. Eugene residents love their trails and often go out of their way, when encountering another hiker, to be helpful and courteous.

What Are "Easy" and "Best"?

Drive any road out of Eugene, whether toward the coast, into the mountains, or even in and around the city, and you will pass trailheads every few miles. In Lane County alone, you could probably hike a different trail every weekend for twenty or thirty years and never repeat yourself. Throw in the trails one county north—around the Santiam River, Opal Creek, Bull of the Woods Wilderness, and Mount Jefferson—or one county south, around the North and South Umpqua Rivers, Mount Thielsen, and Crater Lake National Park—and you could hike a trail a week for a lifetime and not run out.

Because of the sheer quantity of trails, settling on a select few that stand out among all others as both "easy" (actually, "easy to moderate") and among the very "best" was a challenge—especially since both "easy" and "best" are rather subjective terms. The good news is that nearly every trail in this book fairly leapt out at the authors and demanded to be included.

In a few cases, only a portion of a trail met the "easy" and "best" criteria. That does not mean that the unselected portion, presented as an "option," isn't excellent; it simply means that the selected portion is not to be missed. For nearly every hike, multiple options are presented in addition to the described trail. Readers are urged to not only take advantage of them, but also to use this book as a springboard to further explore and develop a lifelong habit of healthy hiking and an appreciation of the outdoors.

Weather

Eugene's climate is fairly mild, with few extremes. The average annual temperature is 53.3 degrees F, the average July maximum is 82, and the average January minimum is 32. Although there is almost no summer rain, the city experiences 209 cloudy days per year. Hiking in and near the city is fantastic in spring, summer, and fall (although the sun can be oppressive when hiking in low-lying open areas in summer). In winter, the rain, fog, and overcast can also be oppressive. From November through mid-June, expect snow above 3,500 feet elevation. No matter what the season, it is usually cooler and rainier near the coast and up in the mountains than it is in Eugene. However, in spring and fall, when hiking in lush, low-elevation river canyons (especially near the coast), even when it's only 65 or 70 out, the humidity can approach 100 percent and cause you to perspire as though it was much warmer.

Day Hiking Tips

One nice thing about easy day hikes is that they don't require as much preparation as difficult overnight hikes. Still, you can get into trouble even on a short hike, and some basic knowledge and precautions can be life-saving. Here is a sampling of the most important things to know:

- **Water.** Always carry water, even on short hikes in cool weather. A couple bottles of store-bought water or a reusable bottle filled with water from home, stashed in a light day pack, will usually keep you quenched and happy no matter how hot it gets, especially on the relatively easy trails in this book. Should something unexpected happen and you find yourself stranded, the extra water could save your life. Remember that nearly every bad thing that can happen on a trail is made worse by dehydration. A sure sign of early dehydration is bright yellow urine.

- **Mosquitoes.** Mosquitoes are worst near standing water and near snowmelt patches (they breed in the puddles). As the season dries up, they tend to go away. The biggest mosquito problem in this book is on the Erma Bell Lakes Trail (Hike 20). If you go before mid-August, bring insect repellent. After August, they're pretty much gone.

- **Clothing.** Dress comfortably and according to your personal taste. In "hypothermia weather" (any season other than summer), loose and layered clothing traps heat better than tight clothes. Rain gear and fleece/down can be invaluable in helping retain body heat in hypothermia weather. Always bring a jacket, no matter what, because if something happens and you have to unexpectedly spend the night, you'll need it, even in summer. Shoes should be comfortable; for the trails in this book, a heavy hiking boot is probably unnecessary (although a sturdy high-top boot can help prevent a sprained or broken ankle).

- **Sun protection.** In summer, in open or mostly open areas, hats, sunglasses, and sunscreen are essential. Sunburn is not a trifling matter. First of all, it is very dehydrating and energy-sapping. Also, a bad sunburn while in your twenties can turn into malignant melanoma forty years later, which is potentially fatal.

- **Bears and cougars.** Bears and cougars can get aggressive, but your chances of seeing one on these trails is so remote as to barely merit consideration—except possibly at the Erma Bell Lakes trailhead, where a sign warns of a bear hanging around the parking lot and breaking into cars. The rangers' advice? Don't leave food in your car that is visible through the window. While hiking, make a little noise once in a while, especially just before rounding a bend. Just a little noise will do—you don't want to bothers other hikers. (See Leave No Trace.) If the animals hear you coming, they'll be long gone by the time you get there, since they wish to avoid encounters as much as you do.

- **Food.** The best trail foods contain high carbs and high water content. Most of all, avoid foods that are difficult to chew and that require lots of saliva (steak and peanut butter are out), and foods that are difficult to digest (such as fried eggs). Sliced fruit is fantastic (less chewing uses up less energy). So are nuts, trail mix, energy bars, juice, thinly sliced cheese, thinly sliced meat, Gatorade, and the usual assortment of traditional trail foods.

- **Overheating and hypothermia.** Two lurking dangers on any hike are overheating and underheating. Overheating can lead to heat exhaustion and heat stroke, while underheating can lead to hypothermia. For heat exhaustion (symptoms include headache, dizziness, nausea, breathlessness, profuse sweating), rest, get out of the sun, and drink water until you feel better. For heat stroke (headache, dizziness, fever, and very little sweating), immediate medical attention is required, although the first-aid treatment is similar to heat exhaustion.

With heat stroke, the body loses its ability to produce perspiration and regulate its temperature. Ideally, you will rest, get out of the sun, and take a drink long before either condition develops.

Hypothermia occurs when the body's heat core begins to cool. The main symptom is uncontrolled shivering. Extreme cold can cause this, but so can moderate temperatures combined with a breeze and perspiration. Always wear a jacket or rain gear to hold in your body heat when it's cool out, even if it's a little uncomfortable to do so.

- **Children.** Taking your children hiking is a great educational and family bonding experience, but it should be done with caution. For a child under the age of six, keep the hikes short and safe (nature trails, etc.). On longer hikes with older children, be aware that children can't pace themselves very well, they get bored easily and can wander off, and they can do foolish and dangerous things when you aren't looking. They may be more interested if a friend comes along. Above all, be flexible.

- **Toxic plants.** Poison oak is abundant at Spencer Butte (Hike 5) and the Ribbon Trail (Hike 6). Identifying poison oak should be the very first thing any West Coast hiker learns. Even if you've never reacted to poison oak before, the allergy can develop without warning and make you very uncomfortable or ill for days. The plant is most toxic when the leaves first come out. Stinging nettles can cause redness, pain, and swelling, but it goes away fairly quickly. The authors didn't see any nettles along the trails in this book, but they can be difficult to spot because unlike poison oak, they are usually mixed in with a jumble of other plants.

- **Snakes.** You might see a rattlesnake, but don't count on it. You'll almost always hear the telltale rattling noise first, but don't step into or over anything without first checking for rattlers. The standard first aid for snake bites is to get to a doctor within two hours if you can. If not, squeeze out as much venom as possible and try to slow your metabolism by resting, so your kidneys can detoxify the poison faster. Snake bites are not usually life-threatening, except for children, the elderly, and people with heart conditions.

- **Bugs.** Yellow jackets, bumblebees, bald hornets, and scorpions can all give you a nasty sting that swells up and can hurt like mad, but the reaction usually doesn't last long. If you are allergic to stings, however, be sure to always carry an EpiPen, antihistamine, or inhaler. Scorpions (the Oregon variety is small and black) live under rocks and rotted wood, so be careful about turning those over.

- **Lightning.** There are occasional lightning storms in the Oregon mountains during the summer, usually in the late afternoon or early evening. Standing in an open area or under a tree at such times is not advised. Thunder and lightning close up can be terrifying, deafening, and possibly knock you over or cause injury (although this is highly unlikely). If you do run into a storm, try to keep warm and, if you have to, find shelter (a rock overhang will do).

- **First-aid kit.** It's always a good idea to have one with you; if nothing else, carry a few Band-Aids and some sterile pads. You might never use them, but they can be incredibly helpful if you ever get a blister between your toes.

- **Communications.** Cell phones are not likely to work in the mountains, but you never know; if you break a leg, it could save your life. Two-way radios can be helpful if you get separated from your fellow hikers. If you get lost, a compass might or might not help (you need to know in which direction the trailhead lies). A GPS is much more helpful, provided you know how to use it to guide yourself from point to point. At the very least, always let someone know where you are going and when you expect to be back.

- **Maps.** Always bring a map (and don't forget your guidebook), even if it is not your first time on the trail.

- **Intoxicants.** When hiking, you should always be as alert and physically "ready" as possible. Hiking while your reasoning, perception, and ability to react are impaired is extremely foolish and dangerous.

- **Conditioning.** Hiking can help get you in shape, but it also helps to already be in shape. If you are not in good condition, make sure your doctor approves hiking as an activity for you, and don't overdo it, especially in summer at low elevations. If you get out of breath, stop and rest. And remember that while uphill gradients are cardiovascular stressors, downhill gradients are orthopedic stressors; you are more likely to trip, sprain an ankle, or develop a blister on the downhill.

- **Personal security.** Although there is no reason to believe that any hike in this book is unsafe, a couple of security precautions can never hurt. First, hiking after dark, and hiking alone, are not advised. On this book's three paths that are lit at night (Hikes 6, 8, and 9), bicycling is a safer night activity than walking. On most national forest trails, although night hiking is allowed, there is an increased chance of bear or cougar encounters. Day or night, if you feel unsafe, consider bringing a friend, a dog, or carrying pepper spray or a tazer (they make pepper spray for bears).

Trail Regulations/Restrictions

Trails in this guide are located in city parks, regional parks, county parks, national forests, Bureau of Land Management (BLM) land, and a national recreation area. None of the trails are located in state parks. The only city, regional, or county park requiring an entry, parking, or trailhead fee is the Buford Park (Mount Pisgah) Arboretum (Hike 12). Federal fee areas in this book are at Salt Creek Falls, Proxy Falls, Erma Bell Lakes, Linton Lake, and the two Oregon Dunes trails. You may pay on-site by the day or purchase one of several annual federal recreation passes, including the Northwest Forest Pass and the Forest Service Annual Recreation Pass. The best annual pass, by far, is the federal Golden Age Passport (now called the "Senior Pass") for people over age sixty-two. The fee is minimal, they are good in nearly every federal-fee area, and they never expire.

Maps

Excellent (and not-so-excellent) detail maps of every trail in this book may be obtained online and printed out. For trails in Willamette National Forest, search the trail name plus "Willamette National Forest," because their maps and trail descriptions may otherwise not show up on the first page of search results. To save you the trouble of searching, pertinent URL web addresses are included under Trail Contacts below and with each hike.

For trails in or near Siuslaw, Umpqua, and Willamette National Forests, recreational forest maps are available at any ranger station, and are indispensable when traveling on forest roads. For trails in and near Eugene, the Eugene Parks and Open Space Department can provide you with a City of Eugene Parks, Recreation and Open Space Map (including the entire Ridgeline Trail), a map/brochure of Hendricks Park, a map/brochure called Ruth Bascom Riverbank Path System (including Pre's Trail at Alton Baker Park), and the West Eugene Wetlands Guide. The Forest Service–operated Oregon Dunes Information Center, in Reedsport, can provide detail maps of trails in the Oregon Dunes National Recreation Area and Siuslaw National Forest (there are many). The BLM-Eugene District has an excellent brochure/map of the Row River Trail.

USGS topographic maps, listed for every trail, are available in outdoors stores and are helpful in showing minute detail and elevation changes. The *DeLorme Oregon Atlas & Gazetteer,* available in outdoors stores and bookstores, also provides useful information in a single volume.

Leave No Trace

The trails described in this book are quite popular and sometimes can take a beating (there's a marathon run every September on the McKenzie River Trail). We, as trail users and advocates, must be especially vigilant to make sure our passage leaves no lasting mark.

These trails can accommodate plenty of human travel if everyone treats them with respect. Just a few thoughtless, bad-mannered, or uninformed visitors can ruin a trail for everyone who follows. The Falcon book *Leave No Trace* is a valuable resource for learning more about these principles.

Three Leave No Trace Principles:

- Leave with everything you brought.
- Leave no sign of your visit.
- Leave the landscape as you found it.

Most of us know better than to litter. It is unsightly, polluting, and dangerous to wildlife. Be sure you leave nothing behind regardless of how small it is. Pack out your own trash, including biodegradable items like orange peels, which might be sought out by area critters. Also, consider picking up trash that others have left behind.

Follow the main trail, Avoid cutting across switchbacks and walking on vegetation beside the trail. For resting spots, select durable surfaces such as rocks, logs, or sandy areas.

Don't pick up souvenirs like rocks, shells, feathers, driftwood, or wildflowers. Removing those items will diminish the next hiker's experience.

Avoid making loud noises that may disturb others. Remember that sound travels extremely well along ridges and through canyons.

Don't smoke on the trail—not only because it impairs your breathing, smells up the area, and could possibly start a forest fire, but also because cigarette butts and filters are unsightly and could harm wildlife.

On a steep trail pitch, the uphill person has the right of way. And if you are standing in the middle of a trail, talking, resting, or taking a picture, step aside if other hikers approach.

Finally, abide by the golden rule of backcountry travel: If you packed it in, pack it out! Thousands of people who come after you will be grateful for your courtesy.

Trail Contacts

Oregon Dunes Information Center / Siuslaw NF
855 Highway Ave.
Reedsport, OR 97467
(541) 271-3611
Hikes 1, 2, and 3

Siuslaw National Forest
4077 SW Research Way
Corvallis, OR 97339
(541) 750-7000
www.fs.fed.us/r6/siuslaw/recreation/ohv/odnra/
Hikes 1, 2, and 3

Mapleton Ranger District / Siuslaw NF
4480 Hwy. 101
Florence, OR 97439
(541) 902-8526
Hike 3

Eugene Parks and Open Space
1820 Roosevelt Blvd.
Eugene, OR 97402
(541) 682-4800
www.eugene-or.gov/parks
Hikes 4, 5, 6, 7, 8, 9, and 10

West Eugene Wetlands Education Center
751 S. Danebo Ave.
Eugene, OR 97402
(541) 683-6998
www.wewetlands.org
Hike 7

Willamalane Park and Recreation District
250 S. 32nd Street
Springfield, OR 97478
(541) 736-4544
www.willamalane.org
Hike 11

Lane County Parks and Recreation
3050 N. Delta Hwy.
Eugene, OR 97408
(541) 682-2000
www.lanecounty.org/departments/pw/parks
Hike 12

Umpqua National Forest
2900 NW Stewart Pkwy.
Roseburg, OR 97470
(541) 672-6601
www.fs.fed.us/r6/umpqua/
Hikes 13 and 14

Cottage Grove Ranger District
Umpqua National Forest
78405 Cedar Park Rd.
Cottage Grove, OR 97424

(541) 942-5591
Hikes 13 and 14

Bureau of Land Management—Eugene District
3106 Pierce Pkwy., Suite E
Springfield, OR 97477
(541) 683-6600
www.edo.or.blm.gov/recreation
Hike 13

Willamette National Forest
211 E. Seventh Ave., Federal Bldg.
Eugene, OR 97440
(541) 465-6521
www.fs.fed.us/r6/willamette/
Hikes 15, 16, 17, and 18

McKenzie Ranger District
Willamette National Forest
Hwy. 126
McKenzie Bridge, OR 97413
Hikes 15, 16, 17, and 18

Oakridge Ranger District
Willamette National Forest
46375 Hwy. 58
Westfir, OR 97492
(541) 782-2291
Hikes 19 and 20

How to Use This Guide

This guide is designed to be simple and easy to use. Each hike is described with a map and summary information that delivers the trail's vital statistics, including length, difficulty, fees and permits, park hours, canine compatibility, and trail contacts. Directions to the trailhead are also provided, along with a general description of what you'll see along the way. A detailed route finder (Miles and Directions) sets forth mileages between significant landmarks along the trail.

Hike Selection

This guide describes trails that are accessible to every hiker, whether they are visiting from out of town or are lucky enough to live in Eugene. The hikes are no longer than 5 miles round-trip, and most are considerably shorter. They range in difficulty from level excursions perfect for a family outing to more challenging hilly treks. While these trails are among the best, keep in mind that nearby trails, often in the same park or preserve, may offer options better suited to your needs.

Difficulty Ratings

These are all easy hikes, but *easy* is a relative term. To aid in the selection of a hike that suits particular needs and abilities, each is rated easy, moderate, or more challenging. Bear in mind that even the most challenging routes can be made easy by hiking within your limits and taking rests when you need them.

- **Easy** hikes are generally short and flat, taking no longer than an hour to complete.

- **Moderate** hikes involve increased distance and slight changes in elevation, and will take one to two hours to complete.

- **More challenging** hikes feature some steep stretches, greater distances, and generally take longer than two hours to complete.

These are completely subjective ratings. What you consider easy is entirely dependent on your level of fitness and the adequacy of your gear (primarily shoes). If you are hiking with a group, you should select a hike with a rating that's appropriate for the least-fit and/or -prepared person in your party.

Approximate hiking times are based on the assumption that on flat ground, most walkers average 2 miles per hour. Adjust that rate according to the steepness of the terrain and your level of fitness (subtract time if you're an aerobic animal, and add time if you're hiking with kids), and you'll have a ballpark hiking duration. Be sure to add more time if you plan to picnic or take part in other activities, like bird watching or photography.

Trail Finder

Best Waterfall Hikes

Best Riverside/Creekside Hikes

Best Open Wetland Hikes

Best Summit Hikes

Best Mountain Lake Hikes

Map Legend

═══⑤═══	Interstate Highway
═══⑩⑪═══	U.S. Highway
═══⑳═══	State Highway
═══F60═══	Minor Road
───────	Local Road
= = = = = =	Unpaved Road
┝━┿━┿━┥	Railroad
▬▬▬▬▬▬	Featured Trail
▬▬▬▬▬▬	Paved Trail
- - - - - -	Trail
∼∼∼	River/Creek
∼ ∼ ∼	Marsh/Swamp
▭	National Forest
▰	Bench
≍	Bridge
▲	Camping
▲	Mountain Peak
🅿	Parking
≻	Pass
🎋	Picnic Area
▪	Point of Interest/Structure
🛉🛉	Restrooms
⌀	Spring
○	Town
⓫	Trailhead
🍃	Viewpoint/Overlook
❓	Visitor/Information Center
≋	Waterfall

Coastal / Florence

1 Oregon Dunes Loop

This fun and fascinating trail involves sliding down the face of a sand dune and then hiking a mile across the sand to the ocean.

Distance: 2.1-mile loop
Approximate hiking time: 1 to 1.5 hours
Difficulty: Easy to moderate
Elevation: 240 to 0 to 150 feet
Trail surface: Soft sand and compacted dirt; the final few hundred feet back to the parking lot are gravel, then asphalt.
Best season: Any. Expect heavy rain and high surf in winter. The trail through the deflation plain may not be passable in winter and spring due to standing water (suggest rubber boots). Ask a ranger at the Oregon Dunes Information Center in Reedsport if the trail is passable.
Other trail users: Heavy use; hikers only
Canine compatibility: Dogs must be leashed. Also, watch for additional temporary pet restrictions,

posted as needed, to protect wildlife.
Fees and permits: Federal parking fee
Schedule: This is a "day use area." The trail is closed and the parking lot is gated from 7 p.m. to 6 a.m.
Maps: Siuslaw National Forest, USGS-Tahkenitch Creek. Excellent detail maps available at the Oregon Dunes Visitor Center in Reedsport.
Trail contacts: Oregon Dunes National Recreation Area, Visitor Center / Siuslaw NF, 855 Highway Ave., Reedsport, OR 97467; (541) 271-3611; and Siuslaw National Forest, 4077 SW Research Way, Corvallis, OR 97339; (541) 750-7000; www.fs.fed.us/r6/siuslaw/recreation/ohv/odnra/

Finding the trailhead: On US 101 between Florence and Reed-sport, near milepost 201, look for the brown turnoff sign marked OREGON DUNES DAY USE. Park in the little loop and walk toward the wooden ramp at the loop's far end. A stop at the excellent Oregon Dunes Information Center in Reedsport is highly recommended. GPS coordinates: N43 49.970, W124 09.108

The Hike

Most trails are designed to be safe and prudent. The Oregon Dunes Trail—at the beginning, at least—is designed to be pure fun. The path's initial segment climbs a stairway to the top of the highest sand dune and then drops abruptly over a nearly vertical (and slightly scary) sand slope down to a trail marker, far below, in the middle of a sandy basin. To get to the marker, you have to slide down the dune face. Don't worry, though; there's an alternate, much easier route back up, which is why this is called a "loop."

The trail follows a classic Oregon Coast dunes profile, beginning in the high and mostly barren dunes and then dropping steeply down to a sandy basin ("deflation plain"), on which there grows a dense but stunted forest. The trail then emerges into a foredune area of much lower dunes, with a fairly dense cover of European beach grass, before reaching the beach.

It is the European beach grass holding the foredune sand in place that created the deflation plain. Fifty years ago, before beach grass invaded the foredunes, the deflation plain and the stunted forest was not present. Now they are found practically everywhere in dune areas along the Oregon Coast.

It is 0.2 mile from the trailhead to the bottom of the big dune and another 0.1 mile to the junction with the 2.5-mile

Tahkenitch Creek Loop side trail. The far end of the rather difficult Tahkenitch Creek Loop is located where the main trail meets the beach.

The soft sand can make it difficult to cross the sandy basin portion of the Oregon Dunes Trail, especially where it slopes gently uphill. The route is marked by wooden posts.

At mile 0.3, the path enters the stunted forest growing in the deflation plain. While the trail remains sandy, it becomes much more firm and level. The deflation plain is a fascinating ecosystem comprised mostly of stunted lodgepole pines (called "shore pines" when found on the coast), a few stunted Sitka spruces, wax myrtle, and lots of Scotch broom. The presence of a little salal in the understory is surprising, because the low, herbaceous species usually indicates rich soil. The deflation plain is an excellent wildlife area, especially in winter. Observant hikers might see bear, deer, bobcat, coyote, raccoon, opossum, pine marten, weasel, chipmunk, squirrel, river otter, and beaver.

At mile 0.9, the path breaks out of the woods, crosses the low, grassy foredunes, and meets the beach, and the far end of the side loop, at mile 1.0.

At mile 1.8 on the way back, near the largest of the wooden posts, the return trail takes off on the left so you don't have to re-climb the dune (although some people do). The return path is gravel at first, and after the final switchback, becomes paved. It emerges at mile 2.1 by the restrooms.

Options: The 2.5-mile Tahkenitch Creek Loop begins at mile 0.3 and ends at mile 1.0. It is a difficult route over the dunes that visits a small creek and follows the beach for a mile.

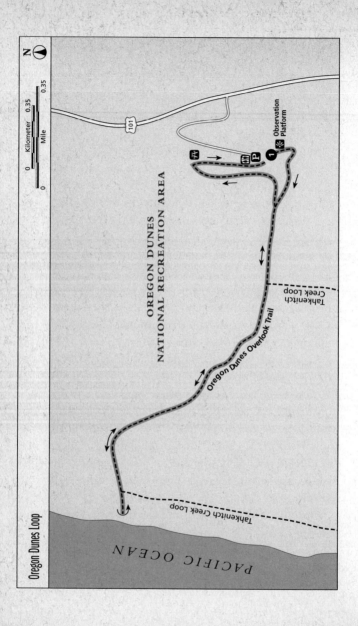

Oregon Dunes Loop

OREGON DUNES
NATIONAL RECREATION AREA

PACIFIC OCEAN

Tahkenitch Creek Loop

Oregon Dunes Overlook Trail

Tahkenitch Creek Loop

Observation Platform

N

Kilometer
0   0.35

Mile
0   0.35

101

Miles and Directions

0.0 The trail begins with a wooden ramp, an observation platform, a stairway, another observation platform and, finally, the actual trailhead, all in less than 0.1 mile.

0.1 From the trailhead at the second observation deck, follow the trail a short way to the top of the highest dune.

0.2 Slide down the sandy dune face to a sandy basin at the base of the high dune.

0.3 You'll pass the beginning of the Tahkenitch Creek Loop trail, on the left, and enter the woods and deflation plain shortly after.

0.9 The trail emerges from the woods onto the low, grassy foredunes.

1.0 The trail ends at the beach. The far end of the Tahkenitch Creek Loop trail comes in on the left, paralleling the beach. This is the turnaround spot to return to the trailhead.

1.8 Back in the sandy basin at the bottom of the high dune, look for a large post marking a gravel side trail on the left that will take you back to the trailhead without having to re-climb the high dune.

2.1 End the hike at the parking area.

2 Taylor Dunes Trail

This is a short, easy hike through the woods and past a small lake to the beginning of a longer and much more difficult trail through the dunes.

Distance: 1.0 mile out and back
Approximate hiking time: 0.5 hour (round-trip)
Difficulty: Easy
Elevation: 100 feet
Trail surface: Gravel
Best season: Any
Other trail users: Hikers only; light to moderate use
Canine compatibility: Dogs must be leashed.
Fees and permits: Federal parking fee
Schedule: Open 24 hours

Maps: Siuslaw National Forest, USGS–Tahkenitch Creek. Excellent detail maps are available at the Oregon Dunes Information Center in Reedsport.
Trail contacts: Oregon Dunes National Recreation Area, Visitor Center / Siuslaw NF, 855 Highway Ave., Reedsport, OR 97467; (541) 271-3611; and Siuslaw National Forest, 4077 SW Research Way, Corvallis, OR 97339; (541) 750-7000; www.fs.fed.us/r6/siuslaw/recreation/ohv/odnra/

Finding the trailhead: Follow US 101 between Florence and Reedsport, near milepost 200, to the brown turnoff sign and side road. The sign says TAYLOR DUNES TRAILHEAD—CARTER DUNES CAMPGROUND. Parking for the trailhead is immediately after the turnoff from the highway, at the end of a short side road on the left. GPS coordinates: N43 51.644, W124 08.525

The Hike

From the parking area, the Taylor Dunes Trail goes through the woods for a few feet, then crosses the access road and enters a beautiful, dense coastal forest of Douglas-fir, Sitka spruce, rhododendron, blackberry, and salal. Hikers arrive at Taylor Lake after 0.1 mile, at a little wooden footbridge across the outlet creek. This is an excellent wildlife observation area with mallard ducks, Canada geese, bald eagles, osprey, and more. The lake covers about an acre and is very marshy and surrounded by lush vegetation.

Beyond the lake, the path winds through the forest for another 0.4 mile, to a sign that says BEACH 3/4 MILE. At the sign, a side trail takes off to the right, leading across an open, sandy basin (the side trail is actually the second portion of the Taylor Dunes Trail). Perhaps 50 feet after the junction with the side trail, the main trail ends at a little wooden viewing platform in the woods that looks out on the sandy basin and the dunes beyond.

The side trail, after 100 feet or so, leads to another viewing spot atop a little hillock in the open, sandy area, with a park bench on top. It then continues on to link with the Carter Dunes Trail and eventually, the beach (See Options).

Options: The sign near the end of the trail that says BEACH 3/4 MILE is fairly accurate. However, hikers should be aware that stated distances for the Taylor and Carter Dunes Trails, as shown on numerous detail maps and online references, vary widely.

Here are the most recent Forest Service measurements: From the end of this hike's "official" route on the Taylor Dunes Trail, at the junction near the overlook at mile 0.5, it is 0.3 mile to the junction with the Carter Dunes Trail. The Carter Dunes Trail is 0.7 mile long. From the Taylor/Carter junction, it is about 0.4 more mile to the beach (turn right) and 0.3 mile back to the Carter Lake Campground (turn left).

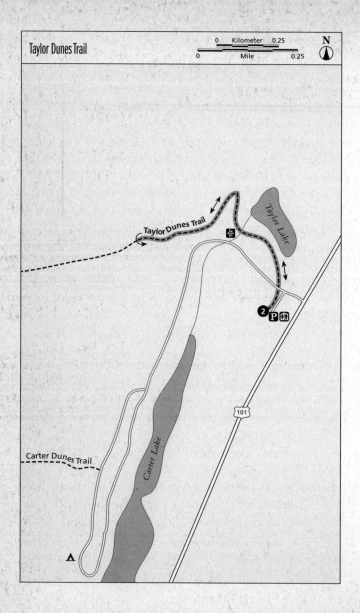

Taylor Dunes Trail

0   Kilometer   0.25

0   Mile   0.25

N

Taylor Dunes Trail

Taylor Lake

2 P

101

Carter Dunes Trail

Carter Lake

The lower 0.3-mile portion of the Taylor Dunes Trail runs through soft sand and is more difficult than the officially described initial 0.5 mile, which is mostly gravel. The Carter Dunes Trail is even more difficult because it climbs some large dunes, and therefore has a difficulty rating of "moderate to difficult."

To drive to the Carter Lake Campground and the Carter Dunes trailhead, continue for 0.5 mile down the access road from the Taylor Dunes parking area.

Miles and Directions

0.0 Park at the Taylor Dunes parking area and begin hiking into the woods at the trailhead. You'll cross the road after 30 feet or so, then reenter the woods.

0.1 The trail arrives at the Taylor Lake footbridge and viewing platform. This is a good spot to linger a bit and look for wildlife.

0.5 The route passes a trail junction on the right with a sign that says BEACH ¾ MILE. The side trail is actually the continuation of the Taylor Dunes Trail. If you go straight, the path ends in 50 feet at a wooden viewing platform. The platform is the turnaround point.

1.0 Arrive back at the trailhead.

3 Sweet Creek Trail/Falls

The Sweet Creek Trail is a lush, magnificent 2.7 mile path in five segments and four trailheads. The described hike covers only the first two segments, with the three others listed as "options." The initial segment, through Sweet Creek Gorge, covers 0.8 mile and passes nine waterfalls, including Annice Falls. The second segment, 0.3 mile, visits only one waterfall, Sweet Creek Falls, the best of the route's eleven waterfalls (but not by much). The next two segments, while extremely pretty, visit no waterfalls and are listed as "options." The fifth and final segment, to Beaver Creek Falls (the eleventh waterfall), is also described as an "option."

Distance: 2.2 miles out and back
Approximate hiking time: 1.5 hours (round-trip)
Difficulty: Easy
Elevation: 153 to 346 feet
Trail surface: Gravel and dirt (plus three areas of metal grating and one wooden footbridge)
Best season: Any. Temperatures are moderated by the ocean in summer, and the site is well below the snow zone in winter. It can be very humid in any season, and extremely wet in fall, winter, and spring. Winter is best for viewing salmon spawning, but the trail can be muddy. Despite these possible inconveniences,

this is a fantastic trail whenever you visit.
Other trail users: Hikers only
Canine compatibility: Dogs must be leashed or under voice control.
Fees and permits: Non-fee parking areas
Schedule: Open 24 hours
Maps: Siuslaw National Forest, USGS–Goodwin Peak
Trail contacts: Oregon Dunes National Recreation Area, Visitor Center / Siuslaw NF, 855 Highway Ave., Reedsport, OR 97467; (541) 271-3611; and Siuslaw National Forest, 4077 SW Research Way, Corvallis, OR

97339; (541) 750-7000; www
.fs.fed.us/r6/siuslaw/recreation/
ohv/odnra/; Mapleton Ranger

District / Siuslaw NF, 4480 Hwy.
101, Florence, OR 97439; (541)
902-8526

Finding the trailhead: From Eugene, take OR 126 (11th Avenue westbound) approximately 45 miles to milepost 15, just outside of Mapleton. As you approach the Siuslaw River Bridge, a sign pointing left, immediately before the bridge, says SWEET CREEK ROAD. Turn left and follow the road for 10 miles (the first 4 miles run parallel to the Siuslaw River, and the last 6 miles parallel Sweet Creek), to a brown road sign marked SWEET CREEK TRAIL. After you turn right into the parking area, another sign identifies it as the HOMESTEAD TRAILHEAD. GPS coordinates: N43 57.467, W123 54.135

The Hike

The 0.8-mile trail through Sweet Creek Gorge is one of the great hidden gems in the Coastal Ranges, and the trail is an engineering feat, with areas of metal grating attached to sheer rock faces. Most of the gorge's eight waterfalls are less than 20 feet high, crashing over a series of low, wide benches into enchanting punchbowl pools. Several are multitiered, and all are lovely. The gorge is lined with perpendicular rock faces covered with moss and maidenhair fern.

The surrounding forest is an archetypal Pacific Northwest west-side (of the Cascade Mountains) forest consisting of immense, wide-based western redcedars, huge old Douglas-firs, and elegant western hemlocks. Hardwoods are mostly bigleaf maple and red alder (no cottonwoods or ash), plus willow, hazelnut, salal, common blackberry, and Douglas maple. Goat's beard moss is everywhere.

During salmon spawning season, watch for fish jumping the many waterfalls in their eternal struggle to make their way upstream to reproduce. In spring and early summer, understory wildflowers such as trillium abound.

The highlight of the gorge comes at mile 0.3, when the trail passes Annice Falls, a lovely fan over a black rock face at the mouth of a side creek. There's often not a lot of water in the side creek, but the falls are about 30 feet high.

Beyond the junction with the path from the Sweet Creek Falls trailhead (you can start the hike at the Sweet Creek Falls trailhead if you like, instead of the Homestead trailhead, but you'll miss the gorge and all its waterfalls), there is only one waterfall, but it's a good one. It is 0.2 mile from the junction to the base of Sweet Creek Falls and another short but rather steep 0.1 mile to a railed observation deck halfway up the falls.

Sweet Creek Falls is a series of four tiers that twists 90 degrees. The highest tier tumbles about 35 feet, and the total drop is about 70 feet. There is a large collecting pool in the middle, where the upper observation deck is located, and another at the base.

During low water, it is theoretically possible to cross the creek and hook up with the trail to Sweet Creek Falls coming in from the Wagon Road trailhead, and then climb up to another railed observation deck on the other side of the creek.

The route from the Homestead trailhead through the gorge to Sweet Creek Falls has a few moderate upgrades, but most come at the prettiest spots, when hikers are too distracted to notice the trail pitch.

Options: It is a 0.5-mile drive from the Homestead trailhead to the Sweet Creek Falls trailhead, and another 0.6-mile drive to the Wagon Road trailhead. At the Wagon Road trailhead, near a little concrete bridge over Sweet Creek, the trail on the far side (to the right) will take you

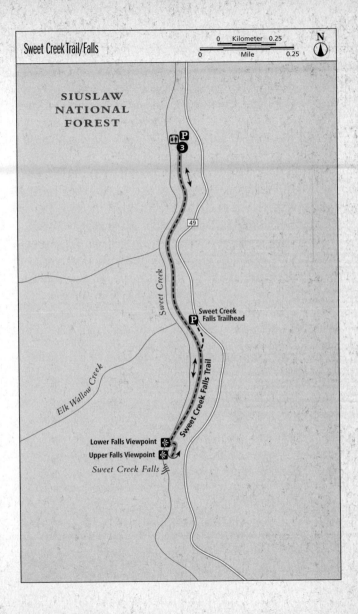

Sweet Creek Trail/Falls

0   Kilometer   0.25
0   Mile   0.25

N

SIUSLAW
NATIONAL
FOREST

P
3

49

Sweet Creek

Sweet Creek
Falls Trailhead

P

Elk Wallow Creek

Sweet Creek Falls Trail

Lower Falls Viewpoint

Upper Falls Viewpoint

Sweet Creek Falls

back to Sweet Creek Falls and the opposite-side observation deck, in 0.8 mile. While very pretty, the gorge trail from the Homestead trailhead is much prettier.

On the near side of the bridge at the Wagon Road trailhead, a trail takes off in the opposite direction (left) that leads up Sweet Creek to Beaver Creek Falls in 0.6 mile. Again, this is a lovely path, but nothing like the initial gorge segment.

Beaver Creek Falls is a must-see, but you can drive almost to the falls. From the Wagon Road Trailhead, continue up the road for 0.2 mile to a turnoff on the left that says BEAVER CREEK FALLS 0.5 MILES. From the little Beaver Creek Falls trailhead (there's parking for perhaps four cars), it is 0.1 mile to the falls, which is actually two falls on two creeks that combine as they tumble. Both fan out over rock faces, and each is about 30 feet high. It's kind of unusual, very pretty, and not to be missed if you're in the area.

Miles and Directions

0.0 Park at the Homestead trailhead and begin the hike into the gorge area.

0.3 The trail passes Annice Falls, coming in on a side creek (look also for a bronze plaque with the name of the falls).

0.8 The trail passes, on the left, the junction with the trail from the Sweet Creek Falls trailhead.

1.0 At Sweet Creek Falls, a short side trail on the right (about 200 feet long) takes you down to the creek and collecting pool. The continuing trail, on the left, makes a sharp, steep, uphill switchback.

1.1 The trail ends at the upper observation deck, with a view of the upper falls and collecting pool. This is the turnaround spot.

2.2 Arrive back at the trailhead.

Eugene / Springfield

4 Mount Baldy / Ridgeline Trail

This short, relatively easy path is considered a highlight of Eugene's 6.3-mile Ridgeline Trail system (except for the side trails up Spencer Butte). While rather steep, it only takes fifteen or twenty minutes to reach the top, and the payoff is outstanding. The summit (elevation 1,232 feet) is level and grassy, with terrific views north and south.

Distance: 1.0 mile out and back
Approximate hiking time: 40 minutes (round-trip)
Difficulty: Easy (it's all uphill but the grades aren't too steep and the route is very short)
Elevation: 975 to 1,232 feet
Trail surface: Aggregate for first two-thirds, and then well-compacted dirt
Best season: Any
Other trail users: Use is light to moderate and for hikers only; a parallel mountain bike path

leads to the same spot.
Canine compatibility: Dogs must be leashed.
Fees and permits: None
Schedule: Eugene city parks are open from 6 a.m. to 11 p.m.
Maps: USGS–Creswell. Excellent detail maps are available from Eugene Parks and Open Space.
Trail contact: Eugene Parks and Open Space, 1820 Roosevelt Blvd., Eugene, OR 97402; (541) 682-4800; www.eugene-or.gov/parks

Finding the trailhead: From the I-5 / 30th Avenue exit (#189), take 30th Avenue west to the light at Hilyard, where you turn left (south). At 33rd Avenue, turn left onto Amazon Parkway East (at light) and continue to Dillard Road, which is just after 43rd Street. Turn left on Dillard and continue for about 2 miles, around a large switchback, up into the hills, and over a crest. The Dillard North trailhead is on the left at the road crest. GPS coordinates: N43 59.911, W123 03.695

The Hike

Immediately south of Eugene, there lies a hilly east-west ridge (called the "South Hills") culminating in Spencer Butte. The 6.3-mile Ridgeline Trail visits much of this ridge, and is accessed by numerous trailheads (Spring Boulevard, Dillard North, Dillard West, Fox Hollow, Willamette Street, and Blanton). Spencer Butte can be accessed either from the Ridgeline system or from its own trailhead.

The second-highest peak in this ridge, after Spencer Butte, is Mount Baldy, named for its dome-shaped, grassy summit. Although 800 feet lower than Spencer Butte (1,232 feet versus 2,055 feet), it is the first notable peak after the ridge rises up from the west bank of the Willamette River.

Of all the segments that comprise the Ridgeline Trail, with the exception of Spencer Butte, Mount Baldy is considered by many to be the most scenic, with the most distinct destination and best vistas. The rest of the Ridgeline Trail is also picturesque and well worth visiting, but Mount Baldy and Spencer Butte are the highlights.

From the parking area, in a grassy opening created by a power line right-of-way, the trail immediately splits into a mountain bike path (right) and a hikers' path (left). The left-hand route quickly enters a dense forest of Douglas-fir where it remains until the approach to the summit.

In July of 2010, workers added some short switchbacks to the path up from the Dillard North trailhead, lengthening the route slightly and making the gradient a little easier. They also put down a layer of aggregate (gravel) to widen and even out the path. The aggregate ends where the trail breaks out of the forest into the open grasslands (interspersed with lupines and daisies), at mile 0.3. The herbaceous vegetation alongside the trail can grow more than 6 feet high here, and although the trail is easy to follow, the panorama may be obscured and you often have to push your way through where the vegetation overtops the trail.

After the long, grassy upgrade, you hit the summit at mile 0.5, where a bench offers an amazing panorama of the city of Eugene. The level, meadowed summit area continues for 0.1 mile. (There is grass on the south side only; the shadier north side is covered in Douglas-fir forest.)

You can have a picnic, linger a while, and enjoy the peaceful panorama; then, return to the trailhead and perhaps try the next Ridgeline Trail segment.

Options: The Dillard West trailhead is 0.5 mile south on Dillard Road from the Dillard North trailhead. The path takes you to the Fox Hollow trailhead after 0.8 mile. If you continue straight ahead at the Baldy summit instead of turning around, it is 0.6 mile farther to the Spring Boulevard trailhead. Climbing Mount Baldy from Spring Boulevard is much steeper than the described route from Dillard North.

Miles and Directions

0.0 From the trailhead parking lot, start up the path and, after about 100 feet, take the left fork for the hiker's trail. The right fork is the mountain bike trail.

0.3 The trail breaks out of the woods into the grasslands and becomes less steep.

0.5 Arrive at the summit, which has forest on the left and grassy meadow on the right. Look for a little wooden bench with a view to the north of downtown Eugene. The level summit area continues for at least 0.1 mile before starting downhill

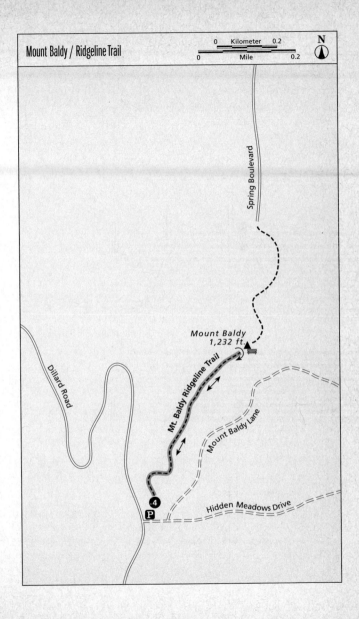

Mount Baldy / Ridgeline Trail

0 Kilometer 0.2
0 Mile 0.2

N

Spring Boulevard

Mount Baldy
1,232 ft.

Mt. Baldy Ridgeline Trail

Dillard Road

Mount Baldy Lane

Hidden Meadows Drive

4
P

on the other side, on its way to the Spring Boulevard trail-head. Turn around either at the bench, in the meadow, at the far end of the mountain bike trail, or where the route starts downhill.

1.0 Arrive back at the Dillard North trailhead.

5 Spencer Butte

Despite its steepness, the Spencer Butte Trail is included for two reasons: First, it is quite short; and second, it is by far the most spectacular trail that the city of Eugene has to offer. For this reason, it is Eugene's most popular and beloved trail, and is not to be missed. From the beautiful trailhead at Spencer Butte Park, there are two routes to the summit. Both are quite steep, but neither is very long. (You can also reach the summit from a connecting link off the Ridgeline Trail.)

Distance: 2.2 miles out and back, or take the 0.6-mile return loop
Approximate hiking time: 1.5 hours (round-trip)
Difficulty: Moderate with a few challenging spots near the summit. The alternate trail (see "Options") is rated as "more challenging."
Elevation: 1,316 to 2,055 feet
Trail surface: Dirt and bark chips; approaching the summit, the path becomes braided, climbs several short rock faces, and can be indistinct and difficult to follow.
Best season: Any; however, keep in mind that the steep rock faces can be slippery in wet weather (winter and spring), and the summit is a lightning rod.
Other trail users: Hikers only; use is heavy, but users are polite and considerate.
Canine compatibility: Dogs must be leashed.
Fees and permits: None
Schedule: Eugene city parks are open 6 a.m. to 11 p.m.
Maps: USGS–Creswell. Excellent detail maps are available from Eugene Parks and Open Space.
Trail contact: Eugene Parks and Open Space, 1820 Roosevelt Blvd., Eugene, OR 97402; (541) 682-4800; www.eugene-or.gov/parks

Finding the Trailhead: From 29th Avenue and Willamette Street, head south for 3.3 miles to the entrance to Spencer Butte Park, on the left. At mile 2.6, you will pass the Willamette Street trailhead for the Ridgeline Trail, on the left, from which Spencer Butte can also be climbed. GPS coordinates: N43 58.817, W123 16.127

The Hike

From the beautiful stairs and kiosk at the forested trailhead in Spencer Butte Park, two trails take off to the summit. The alternate trail on the left is 0.6 mile long and rises 700 feet. The main trail, on the right, is 1.1 miles long, goes to the same place, and also rises 700 feet. This hike highlights the longer, right-hand trail. Although the gradient (feet of elevation gain per mile) on the longer trail is about half that of the shorter trail, the steepest portions of both lie near the top, when you reach the rocks.

A popular option is to ascend on the longer, less-steep trail and descend on the shorter trail. The only problem is that the beginning of the shorter trail, coming down from the summit, may be a little difficult to find and hard to follow.

From the trailhead, the well-manicured longer path climbs steadily—and occasionally rather steeply—through dense Douglas-fir forest, passing scattered rocky outcrops and small springs. At mile 0.6, the route levels off briefly, enters a grassy meadow, and meets the connection to the Ridgeline Trail on the right. Soon after, in a much more open forest stand, at mile 0.8, the previously wide, well-maintained trail becomes much narrower and less distinct. From there to the summit, the path is a steep scramble up rock faces and boulders, sparsely vegetated meadows, and gravelly slopes. There are few if any trees in this final segment, and it can be strenuous. If you lose the trail, just head uphill.

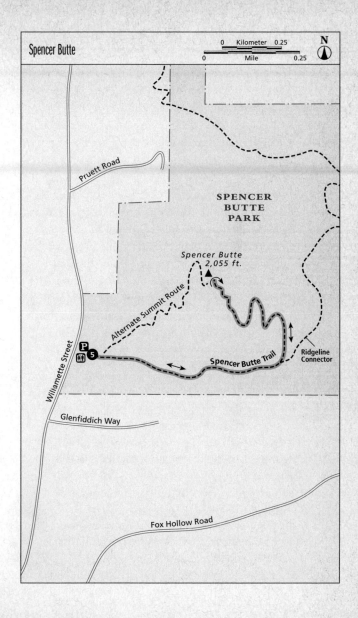

Spencer Butte

0   Kilometer   0.25

0   Mile   0.25

N

Pruett Road

SPENCER
BUTTE
PARK

Spencer Butte
2,055 ft.

Alternate Summit Route

Willamette Street

P 5

Spencer Butte Trail

Ridgeline
Connector

Glenfiddich Way

Fox Hollow Road

The actual summit is a long, narrow rock outcrop about 30 feet high at its highest end. Where the outcrop is only a couple of feet high, climb to the top and make your way along the rocks for the last 100 feet to the actual summit, which is a small, rocky point that can accommodate only about three people (and some hikers tend to hog the spot). The alternate path down begins on the other side of the outcrop. Again, be aware that the summit can be a lightning rod and is not a good place to be during late-afternoon summer thunderstorms.

Options: Again, the shorter, alternate route, beginning on the left at the trailhead, has a much steeper gradient and is far more difficult than the longer, highlighted route on the right. The alternate route makes a better path down than up, although it may be difficult to find from the summit.

Also, from the Willamette Street trailhead on the Ridgeline Trail, it is 2.1 miles to the summit. Go 1.3 miles east on the Ridgeline Trail, then turn off onto the 0.8-mile connecting trail that meets the Spencer Butte Trail, 0.5 mile from the summit.

Miles and Directions

0.0 From the trailhead kiosk, head right for the long trail and left for the shorter, steeper, "alternate" trail.

0.6 In a little meadow, the trail passes the junction with the Ridgeline Trail connector, from the Willamette Street trailhead.

0.8 The maintained trail ends and the route becomes steeper, rockier, and less distinct.

1.1 Arrive at the summit. Either return the way you came or take the shorter, alternate route down (which can be difficult to find from the summit).

2.2 Arrive back at the trailhead.

6 Ribbon Trail / Hendricks Park

The Ribbon Trail—a marvelous little path along a densely forested ravine, smack in the middle of Eugene—feels for all the world like remote wilderness. The route ends at the south end of Hendricks Park, the oldest park in Eugene. From the far end of the Ribbon Trail, to reach the park's main parking lot and primary attractions (the Rhododendron Garden and the Native Plant Garden), you have a choice of four different trails.

Distance: 1.6 miles out and back. For a shuttle hike, leave a car in Hendricks Park and add about 0.5 mile to the Ribbon Trail's one-way length.

Approximate hiking time: 40 minutes (round-trip)

Difficulty: Easy

Elevation: 666 to 839 feet

Trail surface: Aggregate

Best season: Any

Other trail users: This is a popular jogging and dog-walking route.

Canine compatibility: Dogs must be leashed.

Fees and permits: None

Schedule: Eugene city parks are open 6 a.m. to 11 p.m.

Maps: USGS–Eugene East; Hendricks Park brochure

Trail contact: Eugene Parks and Open Space, 1820 Roosevelt Blvd., Eugene, OR 97402; (541) 682-4800; www.eugene-or.gov/parks

Finding the trailhead: From exit 189 on I-5, head west on 30th Avenue for about a mile to the second exit, which is Spring Boulevard. At the end of the off-ramp, instead of turning left onto the overpass to Spring Boulevard, park at the small road stub on the right between the off-ramp and the on-ramp. There is a locked gate there and room for about six cars. Walk around the gate and proceed straight ahead for about 150 feet, until you see a black metal post pointing to the Ribbon Trail, with its gray gravel surface, taking off at a right angle on the right. GPS coordinates: N44 01.397, W123 03.597

The Hike

This is truly a hidden gem amid the hustle and bustle of Eugene. From the 30th Avenue Freeway, and even from the small parking area between the Spring Boulevard off-ramp and on-ramp, there is no indication of a trailhead. Only after following an old closed-off dirt road for about 150 feet do you arrive at the trailhead marker and trail.

The path heads steeply downhill in a broad switchback for 0.2 mile, finally straightening out and turning north. A side trail at mile 0.3 leads into a residential neighborhood. The main trail runs through a dense, moist forest of young Douglas-fir, red alder, and Oregon ash, with an understory of common blackberry, Himalayan blackberry, salal, and numerous wildflowers (and a little poison oak, mostly in the form of climbing vines rather than bushes).

The occasional Oregon white oaks tell an interesting story. For generations, the local natives burned the forest to improve deer habitat. White oak is a tree that grows in dry, grassy areas where there are few or no other trees. After the natives left, the original Douglas-fir forest reasserted itself and the white oak savannah vanished, except for a few large remnant trees.

At about mile 0.5, the path starts steeply uphill and then levels off. At mile 0.7, it heads back downhill, joining the Hendricks Park trail system at mile 0.8.

Options: Hendricks Park covers sixty-one acres and was donated to the city by the Hendricks family in 1906. Three park trails converge at the Hendricks Park end of the

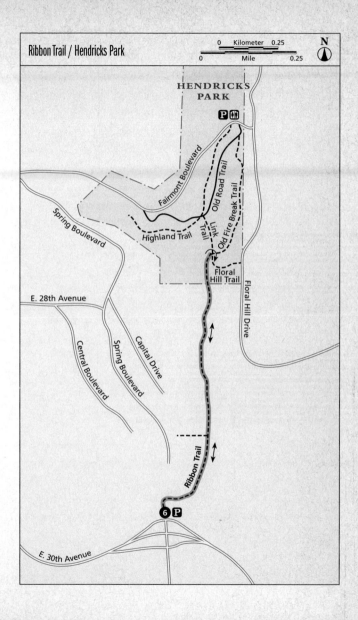

Ribbon Trail / Hendricks Park

0   Kilometer   0.25
0   Mile   0.25

N

HENDRICKS PARK

Fairmont Boulevard

Spring Boulevard

Highland Trail

Old Road Trail

Link Trail

Old Fire Break Trail

Floral Hill Trail

Floral Hill Drive

E. 28th Avenue

Central Boulevard

Spring Boulevard

Capital Drive

Ribbon Trail

6

E. 30th Avenue

Ribbon Trail. If you go 500 feet on the left-hand path, you will arrive at another junction from which you can take four different trails (the Old Road Trail, the Pileated Trail, the Wildflower Trail, and the Highland Trail). It's another 1,500 feet on the Old Road Trail to the F. M. Wilkins Shelter, Rhododendron Garden, Native Plant Garden, and main parking lot on Fairmont Boulevard.

Miles and Directions

0.0 Park at the road stub on the Spring Boulevard on/off ramp and follow the gravel road straight ahead for 150 feet to the actual trailhead.

0.3 Turn right when you come to a black signpost marking the beginning of the Ribbon Trail.

0.8 The trail ends just past the park boundary (unmarked). Either head back or follow one of the three trails that connect the end of the Ribbon Trail to the Hendricks Park trail system (the left-hand fork is recommended).

1.6 Arrive back at the trailhead.

7 Fern Ridge Path / Meadowlark Prairie

This is one of Eugene's best trails—a paved 2.8-mile path through the vast restored wetlands immediately west of Eugene, including the Willamette Daisy Meadow and Meadowlark Prairie. The route crosses creeks, drainage canals, ponds, and marshes, with fantastic wildlife and wild-flower viewing.

Distance: 2.8 miles (one-way shuttle, with a car at the far trailhead)

Approximate hiking time: 1 hour, 15 minutes (one-way)

Difficulty: Easy

Elevation: 400 feet

Trail surface: Wide and paved (concrete), with streetlights

Best season: Any; However, there is no shade whatsoever, and this low-elevation area is humid, so midsummer afternoons probably aren't ideal; bring water and sunscreen.

Other trail users: Hikers, joggers, bicyclists, and in-line skaters

Canine compatibility: Dogs must be leashed.

Fees and permits: None

Schedule: Eugene bike paths are open 24 hours (well-lit at night).

Maps: West Eugene Wetlands Guide; USGS–Eugene West.

Trail contacts: Eugene Parks and Open Space, 1820 Roosevelt Blvd., Eugene, OR 97402; (541) 682-4800; www.eugene-or.gov/parks; West Eugene Wetlands (City of Eugene, US Army Corps of Engineers, Bureau of Land Management, and The Nature Conservancy), West Eugene Wetlands Education Center, 751 S. Danebo Ave., Eugene, OR 97402; (541) 683-6998; www.wewetlands.org

Finding the trailhead: For the South Danebo Avenue trailhead, go west on 11th Avenue from central Eugene (it's one-way for quite a while), which eventually becomes OR 126 to Florence and the coast. It's about 3 miles on 11th from Willamette Street to Beltline Highway.

Danebo is the next light after Beltline. Turn right on Danebo and the trailhead is right there, on the left (There's also a trailhead on the right, heading in the opposite direction, but the described route goes to the left). About 200 feet up the road, on the right, look for the driveway to the West Eugene Wetlands Education Center, where you can park. For the Meadowlark Prairie Overlook, at the trail's far end, get back on OR 126 West and proceed 1.8 miles to the second light, which is Green Hill Road. Turn right and continue 0.3 mile to the overlook, across from the Humane Society. GPS coordinates (South Danebo Avenue access): N44 02.954, W123 10.696

The Hike

This unusual hike may be the best in the immediate vicinity of Eugene. As the paved, well-lit route makes its way through 2.8 miles of wetlands and along creeks and canals, it crosses six concrete footbridges and passes ten wildlife viewing spots with benches and interpretive signs.

The first highlight is the beginning of the Tsanchiifin Nature Trail, a short loop trail with even better wildlife viewing. At Terry Street (mile 0.5), the route passes a private company and parking lot, then crosses an automobile bridge over the Amazon Creek Diversion Channel. The trail then turns right and parallels the channel for 0.5 mile before crossing it and paralleling it for another 0.2 mile. After that, the route veers away from the main channel toward some residences, but the focus is always on the grassy wetlands (the grass is called "tufted hairgrass"), channels, and marshes, while crossing four more footbridges. At mile 2.0, the trail begins to parallel Royal Avenue. At mile 2.2, it makes a 90-degree left turn and parallels Green Hill Road for the final 0.6 mile.

At the Meadowlark Prairie Overlook, where the trail ends, be sure to glance up at the skyline to enjoy the excellent view of the Three Sisters Mountains, the highest peaks in the Central Oregon Cascades. Wildlife in the area includes blue-winged teal, pintail duck, Canada goose, osprey, kingfisher, bald eagle, western meadowlark, river otter, beaver, raccoon, and much more.

Options: The Fern Ridge Path actually begins at the Lane County Fairgrounds on 13th Street, 4.0 miles east of the Danebo Road crossing. While the first 4.0 miles are outstanding (although fairly urban), the scenery ratchets up considerably in the wetlands west of South Danebo Avenue.

The Tsanchiifin Nature Trail is 0.5 mile long and an unpaved side loop off the Fern Ridge Path. It begins soon after the Danebo trailhead and leads to a viewing platform, then back to the main trail.

Miles and Directions

0.0 For the South Danebo Avenue entrance to Fern Ridge Path, park at West Eugene Wetlands Education Center, a couple hundred feet up the road on the right. Cross the road to the trailhead and pass the turnoff to Tsanchiifin Nature Trail.

0.2 Pass the far end of the Tsanchiifin Nature Trail.

0.5 The trail passes an oddly out of place looking private company with "no trespassing" signs, then crosses the Terry Street Bridge. Turn right just over bridge.

1.0 A footbridge crosses the Amazon Creek Diversion Channel, which the path had been following and continues to follow.

1.2 Here is where the path finally leaves the Amazon Creek Diversion Channel and heads out over the open, pond-dotted meadows.

1.8 The route passes the Royal Avenue parking area and trail access.

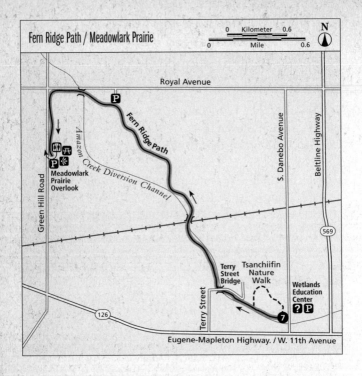

Fern Ridge Path / Meadowlark Prairie

Royal Avenue

Fern Ridge Path

Amazon Creek Diversion Channel

Meadowlark Prairie Overlook

Green Hill Road

S. Danebo Avenue

Beltline Highway

569

Terry Street Bridge

Tsanchiifin Nature Walk

Wetlands Education Center

Terry Street

126

7

Eugene-Mapleton Highway. / W. 11th Avenue

2.0 After crossing another footbridge, the path begins paralleling Royal Avenue.

2.2 Here the route makes a 90-degree turn to the left and parallels Green Hill Road for the remainder of its length.

2.8 The trail ends at the Meadowlark Prairie Overlook, which has parking, picnic tables, and portable toilets.

8 Ruth Bascom Riverbank Path / East Bank (Delta Ponds)

This is a short, easy hike on a well-lit, paved path, featuring a beautiful promenade along the Willamette River at the back end of the Valley River Center shopping mall (Eugene's largest). It then follows the river to the Delta Ponds wildlife area.

Distance: 2.0 to 2.8 miles out and back (depending on where in the shopping mall parking lot you park and start walking)

Approximate hiking time: 45 minutes to 1 hour (round-trip)

Difficulty: Easy

Elevation: 400 feet

Trail surface: Concrete

Best season: Any

Other trail users: Heavily used by hikers, runners, and bicyclists

Canine compatibility: Dogs must be leashed.

Fees and permits: None

Schedule: Eugene bike paths are open 24 hours (well-lit at night).

Maps: Eugene Parks and Open Space Ruth Bascom Riverbank Path map; USGS–Eugene East

Trail contact: Eugene Parks and Open Space, 1820 Roosevelt Blvd., Eugene, OR 97402; (541) 682-4800; www.eugene-or.gov/parks

Finding the trailhead: From I-105 West, in Eugene, follow signs to the Valley River Center mall. After several turns, as you approach the mall on Valley River Drive, turn left at the traffic light to enter the mall parking lot, with motels on the left. Follow this short road until it ends, bearing right into the large parking lot along the rear of the shopping mall. You will see the bike path and promenade running for 0.4 mile along the far edge of the parking lot, alongside the Willamette River.

Park immediately and start walking along the river and parking lot for a 2.8-mile hike (out and back), or drive 0.4 mile to the stop sign at the opposite end of the parking lot, still near the river, to the Greenway Footbridge, for a slightly shorter hike.

The Greenway Footbridge is posted mile marker 0.0 for all four segments of the Ruth Bascom Riverbank Path System. The four segments are: The 2.8-mile East Bank Path (this hike); the 5.0-mile North Bank Path; and across the bridge, the 2.1-mile West Bank Path and the 4.0-mile South Bank Path. GPS coordinates (at the beginning of the Valley River Center parking lot): N44 03.929, W123 06.245

The Hike

(**Note:** This trail has posted mile markers on the ground every quarter mile. However, the route described in this book does not begin where the markers begin and does not end where the markers end. Therefore, the markers do not correlate with the GPS distances tracked from the beginning of the hike. This description gives only the GPS distances.)

If you park at the very beginning of the parking lot and start walking from there, you will find yourself on a lovely promenade along the Willamette River. The path offers excellent views of the river and many short dirt side paths heading down to the water. Away from the mall area, visitors are not permitted to walk down to the water because of wildlife habitat protection. Look mostly for black cottonwood and bigleaf maple trees along this route.

At mile 0.4 from the beginning of the hike, you will arrive at the Greenway Footbridge (posted on the ground as MILE 0.0). That is where the East Bank Path actually starts. (Up to now you've been on the tail end of the North Bank Path.) Shortly beyond the Greenway Footbridge, the path

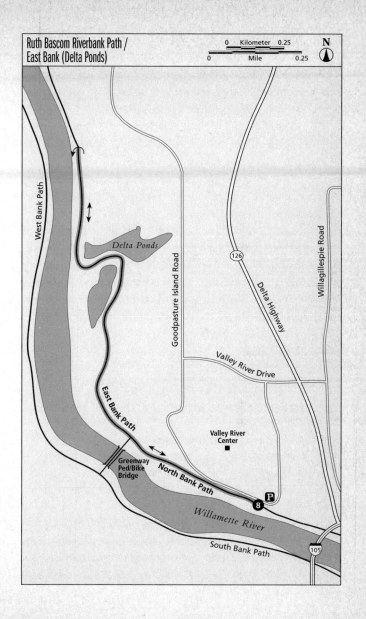

Ruth Bascom Riverbank Path /
East Bank (Delta Ponds)

0   Kilometer   0.25

0   Mile   0.25

N

West Bank Path

Delta Ponds

Goodpasture Island Road

126

Delta Highway

Willagillespie Road

Valley River Drive

East Bank Path

Valley River
Center

Greenway
Ped/Bike
Bridge

North Bank Path

8 P

Willamette River

South Bank Path

105

leaves the river and starts making its way around the first of the Delta Ponds, a low-lying, backed-up wetland. The water is full of algae and aquatic vegetation and is not pretty (but it smells OK). Alert visitors may see mallard ducks, blue herons, bald eagles, pond turtles, and more.

At mile 0.9, the path crosses the top of the concrete outlet gate for the main pond. At mile 1.2, the route leaves the ponds area and begins hugging the riverbank again, passing the beautiful landscaped gardens of a large senior residence. The turnaround is at mile 1.4 from the beginning of the hike (by mile marker 1).

Options: Continue on as you see fit for the path's entire 2.8 miles, with the river on one side and buildings (including Marist High School) on the other. The ponds are definitely the highlight of this path. The two paths on the other side of the Greenway Footbridge are just a little more urban and slightly less scenic than the described route, but also excellent.

Miles and Directions

0.0 Park at the beginning of the Valley River Center parking lot along the Willamette River and start hiking along the edge of the parking lot on the river promenade. You are on the North Bank Path here.

0.4 Arrive at the Greenway Footbridge, which is the end of the North Bank Path and the beginning of the East Bank Path. Continue straight ahead on the East Bank Path.

0.9 Winding through the ponds area, the trail passes the Delta Ponds outlet.

1.2 The trail leaves the Delta Ponds area and continues along the river.

1.4 Turn around and return to the trailhead (at mile marker 1), or continue on.

2.8 Arrive back at the trailhead.

9 Ruth Bascom Riverbank Path / North Bank (Alton Baker Park)

This 2.0-mile segment of the 5.0-mile North Bank Path follows the Willamette River through Alton Baker Park, Eugene's largest park. The park entrance area, with its duck ponds and the DeFazio Footbridge, makes an outstanding starting point. The turnaround is located at the Knickerbocker Footbridge, near the I-5 overpass.

Distance: 4.0 miles out and back
Approximate hiking time: 1.5 hours (round-trip)
Difficulty: Easy
Elevation: 450 feet
Trail surface: Asphalt
Best season: Any
Other trail users: Heavily used by hikers, runners, and bicyclists
Canine compatibility: Dogs must be leashed.
Fees and permits: None
Schedules: Eugene bike paths are open 24 hours (well-lit at night). However, Alton Baker Park, the parking area for this hike, is closed and gated from 11 p.m. to 6 a.m.
Maps: Eugene Parks and Open Space Ruth Bascom Riverbank Path map; USGS–Eugene East
Trail contacts: Eugene Parks and Open Space, 1820 Roosevelt Blvd., Eugene, OR 97402; (541) 682-4800; www.eugene-or.gov/parks

Finding the trailhead: The easiest route to Alton Baker Park is from Franklin Boulevard. Follow it north until it merges with Broadway, then follow signs to Coburg Road over the Ferry Street Bridge. Immediately over the bridge, a sign on the right will say MLK (Martin Luther King Boulevard). Get off there and turn right at the first light (where the sign says CLUB DRIVE). The entrance to Alton Baker Park (Day Island Road) is off Club Drive on the left, immediately after the turn.

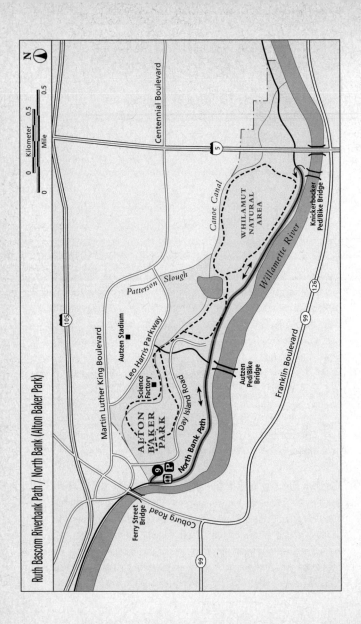

Ruth Bascom Riverbank Path / North Bank (Alton Baker Park)

Once in the park, park and head toward the restrooms. GPS coordinates: N44 03.381, W123 04.876.

The Hike

(**Note:** This trail has posted mile markers on the ground every quarter mile. However, the route described in this book does not begin where the markers begin and does not end where the markers end. Therefore, the markers do not correlate with the GPS distances tracked from the beginning of the hike. This description gives only the GPS distances and disregards the mile markers.)

From the parking area in Alton Baker Park, walk toward the restrooms and then past the duck ponds to the river. The trail starts at the DeFazio Footbridge (named for Peter DeFazio, longtime US congressman from Eugene). Turn left onto the paved bike path and pass posted mile marker 1.75 soon after (it is 1.75 miles from this marker to the Greenway Footbridge behind Valley River Center).

This entire route is shaded and follows the riverbank. Trees are cottonwood, bigleaf maple, and Oregon ash. Occasional dirt side trails lead down to the river.

At mile 0.9 (from the restrooms), the route passes under the Autzen Footbridge. This bridge mostly provides a pedestrian shortcut from the main University of Oregon campus, over the river, and across the park to Autzen Stadium, where the U of O football team plays its home games. A paved pedestrian path leads from the bridge to the stadium.

At mile 1.0, the North Bank Path merges with a wider asphalt path, one of numerous paved walkways that crisscross the park. The route leaves the wider path at mile 1.3 from the restrooms. The remainder of the route is more open as it traverses the area between the river and the high, unmowed grassy fields of the Whilamut Natural Area. Mile maker 3 is passed at 1.5 miles from the restrooms and the route arrives at the Knickerbocker Footbridge at mile 2.0 from the restrooms (just past mile marker 3.5), with the I-5 bridge over the Willamette immediately after. The footbridge is the designated turnaround spot for the described route.

Options: Beyond the Knickerbocker Footbridge, the path goes under the freeway and continues for another 1.5 miles, some of it through urban areas and along roads. Back at the DeFazio Footbridge (mile 0.1), should you decide to head right on the Riverbank Path instead of left, you will find yourself in an extremely narrow strip between I-105 and the river. As indicated, it is 1.75 miles from the DeFazio Footbridge to the Greenway Footbridge.

Miles and Directions

0.0 Park and walk to the restrooms by the duck ponds. You will see the DeFazio Footbridge on the other side of the pond. Walk toward the river.

0.1 When you arrive at the river, turn left onto the paved path and continue hiking.

0.2 The route passes mile marker 1.75.

0.9 The route passes under the Autzen Footbridge.

1.0 The route merges with a paved jogging path.

1.3 Look for a paved path taking off on the right and continuing along the river. This is the continuation of the North Bank Path.

1.5 The route passes posted mile marker 3.

2.0 Arrive at the Knickerbocker Footbridge. This is the designated turnaround spot.

4.0 Arrive back at the restrooms.

10 Pre's Trail Loop (Alton Baker Park)

Pre's Trail is a popular and nationally famous 4.1-mile loop (made up of three loops) that explores virtually every corner of Alton Baker Park, Eugene's largest.

Distance: 4.1-mile loop

Approximate hiking time: 1.5 hours

Difficulty: Easy

Elevation: 450 feet

Trail surface: Orange bark chips

Best season: Spring, summer, fall (a little wet in winter)

Other trail users: Use is extremely heavy by runners and hikers (no bicyclists)

Canine compatibility: Dogs must be leashed (however, the trail passes a leashless pet exercise area).

Fees and permits: None

Schedule: Eugene city parks are open 6 a.m. to 11 p.m.

Maps: Eugene Parks and Open Space Ruth Bascom Riverbank Path map; USGS–Eugene East

Trail contact: Eugene Parks and Open Space, 1820 Roosevelt Blvd., Eugene, OR 97402; (541) 682-4800; www.eugene-or.gov/parks

Finding the trailhead: The easiest route to Alton Baker Park is from Franklin Boulevard. Follow it north until it merges with Broadway, then follow signs to Coburg Road over the Ferry Street Bridge. Immediately over the bridge, a sign on the right will say MLK (Martin Luther King Boulevard). Get off there and turn right at the first light (where the sign says CLUB DRIVE). The entrance to Alton Baker Park (Day Island Road) is off Club Drive on the left, immediately after the turn.

Look for a small sign pointing left as you approach the main parking lot (near the restrooms) that says PRE'S TRAIL. Park and walk to the informational kiosk at the trailhead. GPS coordinates: N44 03.364, W123 04.821

The Hike

(**Note:** Following the entire route is rather complex and involves twelve trail junctions. See Miles and Directions for more information.)

Among the millions of running and jogging enthusiasts in the US, Eugene, or "Tracktown USA," is considered a tourist mecca. And one of the primary attractions visiting runners come to see in Eugene is Pre's Trail.

Steve Prefontaine, for whom the trail is named, was a distance runner who set several records in the 1970s. A track star at the University of Oregon and an Oregon native, "Pre" was tragically killed in a car accident in 1975 at the age of twenty-four. He was an outstanding advocate for U of O and its track program.

The trail begins at the informational kiosk near the main parking lot. Since there are so many junctions, it helps to bring a detail map or guidebook along with you. It is difficult to get lost, however, because no matter where you are in the park, it is always obvious which direction leads back to the parking area (west), which leads to the Willamette River (south), which to Autzen Stadium (north), and which to the I-5 overpass (east). Also, the park is riddled with intersecting paved bike paths and other trails, so there are many shortcuts back to the parking lot. For Pre's Trail, follow the orange bark trail surface (there are no signs at any of the junctions).

From the trailhead, the route passes the return end of the loop, on the right, after about 50 feet. After following a diversion canal for 0.2 mile, the path veers right and picks up the Canoe Canal, which it follows for almost 2.0 miles, with Autzen Stadium (where the University of Oregon

Ducks play football) and Eugene Science Factory, the multicolored building located prominently on the left. This segment runs in and out of wooded patches of Douglas-fir, bigleaf maple, black cottonwood, and Oregon ash. It also passes a couple areas of large hazelnut bushes that appear to have once been domestic orchards.

At mile 0.7, the trail crosses a footbridge to the opposite side of the Canoe Canal, then continues along the canal. Continuing past the leashless pet enclosure (just over the footbridge) and along the canal, you arrive at the duck pond at mile 1.1. At mile 1.2, beyond the pond, the path continues along the canal through a fascinating area with extravagant canal-front homes on one side and the Whil-amut Natural Area on the other. The natural area consists mostly of naturally growing tall grass. Turn right at the trail junction just before the I-5 overpass. This will lead to the Knickerbocker Footbridge and the Ruth Bascom River-bank Path, at mile 2.1. Turn right again near the footbridge and return to the trail, heading away from I-5.

Follow the trail along the Willamette River (there are three paralleling trails in this segment, and Pre's Trail is in the middle), with the Whilamut Natural Area to your right. This will return you to the pond (mile 2.7) to complete the first of the three loops. At the other end of the pond, take the trail fork you didn't take the first time, going straight, which will take you through a wooded stand, past the leashless pet area and the footbridge over the canal, thus completing the second loop.

Do not cross the footbridge this time; instead, follow the path along the opposite side of the Canoe Canal from the way you came in, back to the trailhead (miles 3.3 to 4.1). This final segment follows the canal, then winds through

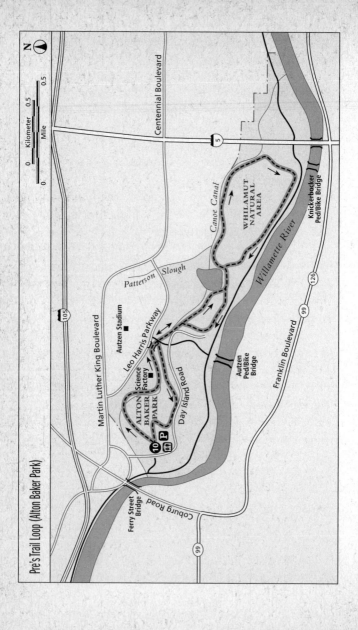

Pre's Trail Loop (Alton Baker Park)

woods and open fields before rejoining the outgoing trail (and completing the third loop) just before the kiosk.

Miles and Directions

0.0 Park and walk to the trailhead kiosk and continue up the trail past the far end of the return loop. Very shortly, the trail will begin following a diversion channel.

0.2 Veer right away from the diversion channel and begin following the Canoe Canal.

0.7 Cross the footbridge over the Canoe Canal near Autzen Stadium and turn left.

0.8 Arrive at a junction; go straight.

1.1 Arrive at the junction just before the pond. Turn left.

1.2 Just past the pond, you will come to yet another junction. Turn left again and rejoin the Canoe Canal.

2.0 As you approach the I-5 overpass, you will arrive at another junction where you will turn right (the trail runs along the side of a paved path).

2.1 Approaching the Knickerbocker Footbridge, turn right and return to the bark path. This will take you along a narrow strip between the river and the natural area, eventually cutting away from the river.

2.7 Arrive back at the pond and turn left at the junction.

2.8 Go straight at the junction at the far end of the pond.

3.1 The trail passes a side trail leading to the Autzen Footbridge; go straight.

3.2 Rejoin the Canoe Canal and turn left at the junction.

3.3 Arrive at the footbridge over the Canoe Canal. Continue straight, past the leashless pet area. Do not cross the bridge.

4.1 Arrive at the end of the loop; turn left and return to the trailhead.

11 Dorris Ranch Loop

This is an easy path that visits a historic, turn-of-the-century ranch, many beautiful old hazelnut (filbert) orchards, and the riparian zone along the Willamette River. There is an excellent river view at the halfway point. The hazelnut farm is still very much in operation.

Distance: 2.2-mile lollipop
Approximate hiking time: 45 minutes to 1 hour
Difficulty: Easy
Elevation: 415 to 464 feet
Trail surface: Chips and dirt (the path is quite wide)
Best season: Any
Other trail users: Use is moderate; hikers only

Canine compatibility: Dogs must be leashed.
Fees and permits: None
Schedule: Dawn to dusk
Maps: USGS–Eugene East
Trail contact: Willamalane Park and Recreation District, 250 S. 32nd Street, Springfield, OR 97478; (541) 736-4544; www .willamalane.org

Finding the trailhead: The trailhead is easy to find because there is a sign at the main intersection in downtown Springfield. To get there, take I-5 to the OR 126 East / Springfield exit (#195-A). On OR 126, get off at the first exit (City Center). You'll end up heading south on Pioneer Parkway, which becomes Second Street after it crosses Main Street (you will see the Dorris Ranch sign here). At Main Street, proceed straight, through the traffic light, and continue for 0.5 mile to the entrance to the Dorris Ranch Living History Farm. Once through the main gate, head to the right for the trailhead parking area and kiosk. GPS coordinates: N44 01.987, W123 01.199

The Hike

Dorris Ranch was established in 1892 and became the largest hazelnut farm in the nation's top hazelnut-producing state. It is still an operating hazelnut ranch; hence, the name "Living History Farm." The ranch covers 258 acres, 71 of which are planted in hazelnut orchards. The orchards are extremely elegant and stately. The trees are large, funnel-shaped bushes that grow as high as 20 to 30 feet, forming beautiful interconnecting arches between the planted rows.

The beginning of the trail follows an old road through the orchards. At mile 0.3, the route passes a turnoff on the left labeled GEORGE'S LOOP 2 MILES. This is where you will come out when you complete the loop. At mile 0.4, the path leaves the orchards and becomes narrower. The route meets the Willamette River at mile 0.5. You can't see very far up or down the river, but it's still a nice view. The trail makes a 90-degree left turn at the river overlook.

Beyond the overlook, the path makes its way through a dense riparian woods of Douglas-fir, Oregon ash, black cottonwood, and California black oak. Not surprisingly, you will see a few wild hazelnut bushes in the understory.

At mile 1.2, the trail makes a gradual, nearly 180-degree turn and heads back toward the trailhead, following between the orchards, on the right, and the woods, on the left. It rejoins the entry trail at mile 1.9, near a small marshy area, and arrives back at the trailhead at mile 2.2.

Miles and Directions

0.0 Begin hiking along the road from the trailhead parking area, kiosk, and vault toilet.

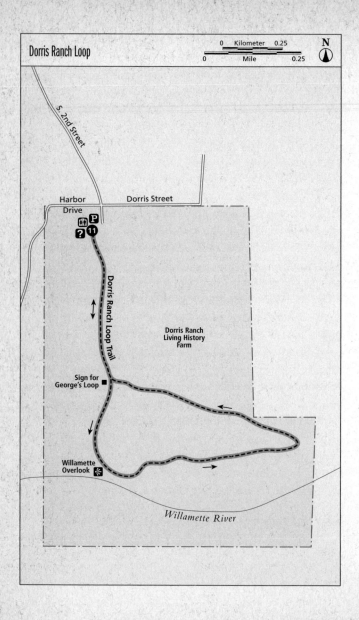

0.3 The route passes the end of George's Loop on the left.

0.5 Leaving the orchards and entering the woods, you arrive at the Willamette River overlook.

1.2 After continuing through the riparian woods, the loop makes a wide U-turn and heads back toward the trailhead, with woods on the left and orchards on the right.

1.9 The loop is completed and the trail emerges onto the entry trail.

2.2 Arrive back at the trailhead.

12 Buford Park (Mount Pisgah) Arboretum Loop

A favorite local hiking place among Eugene and Springfield residents, the maze of trails in the Buford Park Arboretum offers a variety of choices, all excellent and none very long or difficult. For the more adventurous, two trails climb to the summit of Mount Pisgah, also in Buford Park.

Distance: 1.5-mile loop.

Approximate hiking time: 45 minutes

Difficulty: Easy

Elevation: 440 to 570 feet

Trail surface: Bark chips

Best season: Any

Other trail users: Heavy use; hikers only

Canine compatibility: Dogs must be leashed.

Fees and permits: Local parks parking fee

Schedule: Dawn to dusk

Maps: USGS–Springfield/Jasper

Trail contact: Lane County Parks and Recreation, 3050 N. Delta Hwy., Eugene, OR 97408; (541) 682-2000; www.lanecounty.org/departments/pw/parks

Finding the trailhead: Leave I-5 at exit 189 (30th Avenue) and take the side road east of the freeway that goes past the Shell station (road signs point to Mount Pisgah / Arboretum). Immediately after the gas station, turn right on Franklin Boulevard (under the railroad overpass) and right again onto Seavey Loop. (Seavey Loop crosses Franklin twice, so if you miss the first turnoff, turn left at the second turnoff.) Continue for several blocks to where Seavey Loop turns right and Seavey Way continues straight ahead. Follow Seavey Way for 2 more blocks, over the Coast Fork Willamette River and through the park entrance, where it quickly turns right. Stop and pick up a parking permit, then follow Seavey Way for another block or so to where it dead-ends at the arboretum parking lot. GPS coordinates: N44 00.400, W122 58.845

The Hike

(**Note:** The Buford Park Arboretum contains a maze of main paths, side paths, and intersecting roads. To follow the suggested route exactly, bring this book or download a map from the Internet.)

From the parking area, walk past the entrance kiosk and over a small footbridge to another map and kiosk. The large building on the left is the White Oak Pavilion, and the restrooms are on the right. Walk toward the restrooms, following signs to the Tom McCall Riverbank Trail, which also takes you past the Wildflower Garden (a short side loop visits this natural wildflower area). Look for an excellent book of wildflower identification photos alongside the trail.

The Riverbank Trail along the Coast Fork Willamette River is peaceful and charming, shaded by large Oregon ash trees, and features a park bench and overlook. The path emerges at mile 0.3 at Meadow Road and an old barn. Follow Meadow Road (right) for a short distance, past a side road and the junction with the Pond Lily Trail, on the left, to the Water Garden Trail, also on the left.

The Water Garden Trail is recommended as an interesting side loop that ends exactly where you started the loop, on Meadow Road. A lovely footbridge at the far end of the Water Garden Trail offers a shortcut to the far end of the Pond Lily Trail, but if you take it you will miss the Pond Lily Trail (besides, the entire hike is only 1.5 miles so there's not really a need for shortcuts). The Water Garden is an area of natural seasonal wetlands and riparian forest with extremely lush vegetation. It is mostly dry in summer, but there are two small boardwalks to get you through the lingering muddy spots.

Primary woody plant species in the Water Garden area are Oregon ash, black cottonwood, white alder, red alder, willow, red osier dogwood, and snowberry. Herbaceous plants include yellow pond lilies, which grow in the pond along with rushes and sedges, and wildflowers including cow parsnip, wood violet, and larkspur.

Back at the junction of the Pond Lily Trail and Meadow Road, follow the Pond Lily Trail past the pond and the far end of the footbridge, to where the path comes out on the road. Go straight ahead, across the road, following signs for the South Boundary Trail (mile 0.8). This trail quickly takes you past a right-angle turn and overlook, then picks up the Incense Cedar Trail soon after (turn left). The Incense Cedar Trail takes you past the Octopus Tree, an immense, gnarled old incense cedar. Joining the Buford Trail (at mile 1.1), the path leaves the upland forest of Douglas-fir, incense cedar, Oregon ash, and bigleaf maple, and emerges at the edge of an Oregon white oak savannah, with grassy fields and scattered oaks. Passing the White Oak Pavilion, cut across the building grounds and return to the trailhead and parking area (mile 1.5).

Options: There is a shortcut to the Incense Cedar Trail called the Fawn Lily Trail, where the Pond Lily Trail crosses the road and picks up the South Boundary Trail. This may save you a couple of minutes but again, the entire hike is only 1.5 miles and doesn't really need any shortcuts.

Continuing on the South Boundary Trail instead of turning onto the Incense Cedar Trail will lengthen the hike by 0.3 mile, along a route slightly uphill from the Buford Trail. Return via the Zigzag Trail and the Creek Trail.

To climb Mount Pisgah (elevation 1,531 feet), a grassy dome also inside Buford Park, walk to the South trailhead, off the road just outside the arboretum parking lot, or drive to the North trailhead (go north for 0.2 mile instead of south as you enter the park). The North trailhead has its own parking lot, but you'll still need the parking permit. Both the North and the South Trails hit the summit after 1.5 miles and 1,000 feet of elevation gain, which is pretty steep. (Be aware that the summit is not clearly marked on the large maps at the two summit trailheads.)

Miles and Directions

0.0 Within 300 feet of the parking lot, you'll pass an informational kiosk, a footbridge, restrooms, and the beginning of the Riverbank Trail and Wildflower Garden Trail.

0.3 At the far end of the Riverbank Trail, the path emerges onto Meadow Road near the barn. Turn right onto the road and continue past the junction with the side road and the Pond Lily Trail, to the junction with the Water Garden Trail, where you turn left.

0.6 After completing the Water Garden Loop, return to Meadow Road, backtrack a few feet and turn right onto the Pond Lily Trail.

0.8 Emerge from the far end of the Pond Lily Trail at the side road. Follow signs straight ahead to the South Boundary Trail.

0.9 The South Boundary Trail makes a large "L" at an overlook containing a park bench, then joins the Incense Cedar Trail. Turn left onto the Incense Cedar Trail.

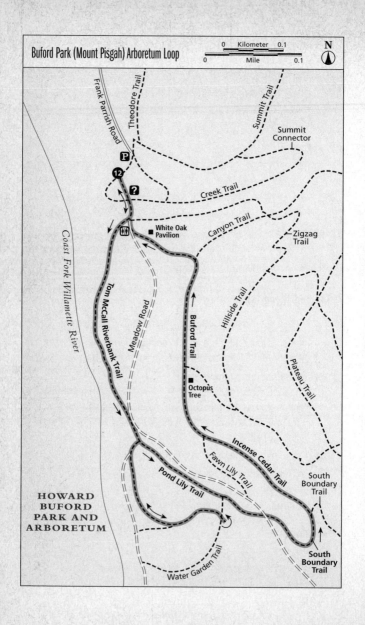

Buford Park (Mount Pisgah) Arboretum Loop

Kilometer 0.1
Mile 0.1

N

Frank Parrish Road
Theodore Trail
Summit Trail
Summit Connector
P
12
?
Creek Trail
Canyon Trail
Zigzag Trail
White Oak Pavilion
Coast Fork Willamette River
Tom McCall Riverbank Trail
Meadow Road
Buford Trail
Hillside Trail
Octopus Tree
Plateau Trail
Incense Cedar Trail
Fawn Lily Trail
South Boundary Trail
Pond Lily Trail
HOWARD BUFORD PARK AND ARBORETUM
Water Garden Trail
South Boundary Trail

1.1 The Octopus Tree is the highlight of the Incense Cedar Trail. Turn left where the Incense Cedar Trail meets the Buford Trail.

1.4 The Buford Trail arrives at the White Oak Pavilion. Cut across the pavilion area and head back toward the trailhead, which is in easy view.

1.5 Arrive at the trailhead, completing the loop.

Cottage Grove

13 Row River Trail

The Row River Trail is a popular, 16-mile biking, hiking, and running path that begins in downtown Cottage Grove, skirts the edge of beautiful Dorena Lake, and then follows the Row River. The path, built in 1994, is part of the Rails to Trails program, in which abandoned railroad tracks are removed and the route is turned into a hiking trail. Before it was torn up, this particular railroad track was featured in the film *Stand by Me*.

This hike describes 2.7 miles of the Row River Trail, from the highway crossing, past Dorena Dam, and along Dorena Lake to Harms County Park. Readers, of course, are free to hike not only the described section but any or all of the remainder of the trail.

Distance: 2.7 miles (one-way shuttle with car at Harms Park)
Approximate hiking time: 1 hour (one-way)
Difficulty: Easy
Elevation: 759 to 925 feet
Trail surface: Asphalt
Best season: Any (may be cold and rainy in winter)
Other trail users: Heavily used by bicyclists and runners
Canine compatibility: Dogs must be leashed.
Fees and permits: None
Schedule: Half an hour before sunrise to half an hour after sunset
Maps: Bureau of Land Management (BLM) brochure–Row River Trail; USGS–Dorena Lake
Trail contacts: Bureau of Land Management—Eugene District, 3106 Pierce Pkwy., Suite E, Springfield, OR 97477; (541) 683-6600; www.edo.or.blm.gov/recreation; Umpqua National Forest, 2900 NW Stewart Pkwy., Roseburg, OR 97470; (541) 672-6601; www.fs.fed.us/r6/umpqua/; and Cottage Grove

Ranger District, Umpqua National   Cottage Grove, OR 97424; (541)
Forest, 78405 Cedar Park Rd.,   942-5591

Finding the trailhead: From the I-5 Cottage Grove exit (#174), head east on Row River Road. Near mile 6, a small street sign pointing left says ROW RIVER ROAD, while the road straight ahead becomes Shore View Drive. Turn left and continue for 1.5 miles to a yellow-green sign indicating a pedestrian and bicyclist crossing. Soon after, you will see the red posts where the Row River Trail crosses the road. There is parking for about five cars just past the crossing, on the right. For the described route, head east (right) on the trail. GPS coordinates: N43 47.509, W122 57.875

The Hike

(**Note:** This trail has posted mile markers on the ground every quarter mile. However, the route described in this book does not begin where the markers begin and does not end where the markers end. Therefore, the markers do not correlate with the GPS distances tracked from the beginning of the hike. This description gives only the GPS distances.)

Most of this path runs through a dense and pleasant forest of small Douglas-fir and large bigleaf maple, with occasional red alder, Oregon ash, and California black oak. There are several open, grassy areas and places where the path comes extremely close to Row River Road, which this segment parallels for its entire distance.

Initially, the path is level, but as it approaches the dam, it starts to gradually ascend, at a grade gentle enough to accommodate a fully loaded freight train. At mile 0.7, where the grade crests, look for a side trail on the right. Following this for 0.1 mile will take you to the top of the dam.

Returning to the main trail, you will immediately pass the Dorena Dam Bureau of Land Management (BLM) parking and access area on the left, with a vault toilet. There's an unmarked trail down to the lake at the toilet.

From just past the dam to the end of the trail, the extremely pretty Dorena Lake is always visible on the right.

You will pass the Row Point BLM parking and access area on the left, at mile 1.2. An easily missed side trail here (on the right) leads down the hill to a grassy area near Row Point, a small forested promontory.

Beyond the Row Point BLM access, the route continues through the woods for another 1.5 miles along the lakeshore. It is mostly level, with a steep slope down to the water. A highlight comes right after Row Point, at a small bay where the trail comes very close to the lake.

Approaching Harms Park at mile 2.7, the path breaks out into the open, almost bumps into the road, and crosses a small footbridge. The described route ends at Harms Park, where there is a vault toilet, parking, picnic tables, and a boat ramp.

Options: The initial 6.0 miles of the Row River Trail, from Cottage Grove, crosses Mosby Creek, the Mosby Creek trailhead, and the Row River; the latter via a covered bridge. This portion of the route runs mostly through grassy fields. The described route is picked up at the road crossing just before milepost 6 (on the trail) and continues past milepost 8 to Harms Park. Beyond that, the path continues along the lakeshore parallel to the road. Past the lake, at milepost 11, it follows the Row River for another 5.0 miles. The road there runs between the trail and the river, and at times, the trail is extremely close to the road.

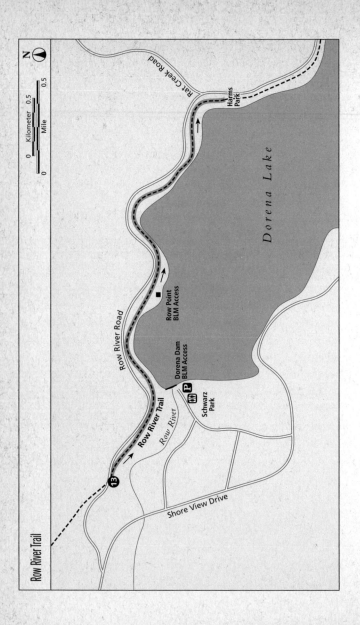

Row River Trail

Miles and Directions

0.0 Begin the route at the road crossing on Row River Road. There's parking for about five cars. Head east toward the lake.

0.7 The trail passes a narrow dirt side trail leading to Dorena Dam. Back on the main trail, shortly after the dam turnoff, you will pass the BLM's Dorena Dam trail access and parking area. There is a vault toilet here.

1.2 The trail passes the Row Point BLM trail access and parking area.

2.7 Arrive at Harms County Park, which has a vault toilet, picnic tables, and a boat launch on Dorena Lake.

14 Bohemia Mountain / Second Saddle

This is a short (0.8 mile, of which the first 0.5 is the "official" route), fantastically beautiful trail in a fascinating historic area, to the top of a craggy mountain. On a clear day, you can see from Mount Shasta to Mount Hood (about 350 miles), one of the best panoramas of the High Cascades. The drive to the trailhead is also outstanding, if a bit challenging.

Distance: 1.0 mile out and back to the second saddle; 1.6 miles out and back to summit. (These distances are difficult to believe because everything seems much farther. However, the map and GPS both show the entire trail as less than a mile each way in horizontal distance.)

Approximate hiking time: 1.5 to 2 hours (round-trip)

Difficulty: Moderate. The trail beyond the described route is extremely difficult.

Elevation: 5,324 to 5,650 feet (summit: 5,987 feet)

Trail surface: Extremely rocky

Best season: Mid-June to mid-Nov

Other trail users: Use is light; hikers only

Canine compatibility: Dogs must be leashed or under voice control.

Fees and permits: None

Schedule: Always open in season. Access roads are impassable due to snow from late fall to late spring.

Maps: Umpqua National Forest; USGS–Fairview Peak

Trail contacts: Umpqua National Forest, 2900 NW Stewart Pkwy., Roseburg, OR 97470; (541) 672-6601; www.fs.fed.us/r6/umpqua/; and Cottage Grove Ranger District, Umpqua National Forest, 78405 Cedar Park Rd., Cottage Grove, OR 97424; (541) 942-5591

Finding the trailhead: From the I-5 exit at Cottage Grove (#174), follow Row River Road east for 16 miles to Sharp's Creek Road. Turn right and follow Sharp's Creek Road for 10.5 miles to the end of the pavement. Turn left there to continue on Sharp's Creek Road. The sign says BOHEMIA MINING DISTRICT / BOHEMIA SADDLE 8 MILES (although it's actually 7.3 miles).

At mile 1.3 after the pavement ends, the gravel road passes Mineral Campground. The next 3.5 miles are extremely steep, twisty, and rocky, requiring a vehicle with high clearance, good tires and suspension, and probably four-wheel drive. Bear left at the major junction at mile 4.8. The final 2.5 miles are also pretty steep and winding, but better than the previous segment.

Park at the saddle. A large sign there indicates the Bohemia Mountain Trail, but you're better off hiking 200 feet down the little road marked by a sign that says TO BOHEMIA SADDLE PARK. Walk up the road to a second, smaller trailhead sign, and pick up the trail there.

If you don't have four-wheel drive, there are two much less challenging routes to Bohemia Saddle, but they are both considerably longer (and also unpaved). Both are also highly scenic. One is reached by continuing straight ahead on Martin's Creek Road, where the pavement ends and Sharp's Creek Road turns left. The route eventually comes out at the junction at mile 4.8 on the upper, unpaved portion of Sharp's Creek Road. Much longer yet is to continue on Row River Road to Brice Creek, following signs to Johnson Saddle and Bohemia Saddle. Consult the Umpqua National Forest map for details on these alternate routes to the trailhead. GPS coordinates (at Bohemia Saddle): N43 34.895, W122 39.346

The Hike

While the Bohemia Mountain Trail absolutely qualifies as a "best" day hike, it is far from "easy." For that reason, the "official" described route ends at the rocky saddle and vista point at mile 0.5 (the second of three saddles that the trail passes). Beyond the second saddle, it's another extremely steep 0.3 mile to the summit, which hikers are encouraged to attempt with the understanding that it is rated by the Forest Service as "most difficult."

A little about Bohemia Saddle and the Bohemia Mining District: The gold and silver mining district has been around since 1866, and still operates hard rock gold mines, mainly on nearby Champion Creek. Much of the Bohemia Mountain Trail is on district property. At the turn of the twentieth century, Bohemia City was located near Bohemia Saddle, but only two buildings remain today.

A side road (sometimes gated) at the saddle leads to the top of Fairview Peak (5,933 feet), which has a 55-foot-tall, still-operating fire lookout tower on top. Bohemia Mountain (5,987 feet), also seen from Bohemia Saddle, rises prominently to the southwest. It is the high, rocky mountain with steep cliffs all around the summit and a flat top.

The Musick Guard Station, just off Bohemia Saddle on the road to Champion Saddle, may be rented for overnight accommodations. The rustic cabin is difficult to see from the road but easily visible from the trail's second saddle.

Bohemia Mountain and Fairview Peak are part of the Calapooya Range, a 60-mile string of ancient volcanoes that are part of the Western Cascades, which lie to the immediate west of the High Cascades. The Western Cascades are much older and far more eroded than the High Cascades (peaks of the High Cascades include the Three Sisters, Mount Shasta, and Mount Hood). The Western Cascades are uniformly marked by an 18-degree tilt to their bedded lava flows, which are horizontal in the High Cascades. Also, there is no gold in the High Cascades.

The most abundant tree along the Bohemia Mountain Trail is Douglas-fir, but you will also find Alaska cedar, an upper-elevation species that is extremely rare in southern Oregon but far more common to the north. You'll also see noble fir, western hemlock, and western white pine. Shrubs include bittercherry and rhododendron (which blooms spectacularly in late June and early July). Herbaceous plants include Oregon bleeding heart, bear grass, Indian paint-brush, lupine, trillium, and much more.

On the trail, a sign at the second trailhead (200 feet up the side road) says that the trail is 0.75 mile long and rated as "most difficult." The steep, rocky pathway follows a wooded ridgetop for a while, then crosses some steeply sloping scree fields before emerging at the first saddle (about mile 0.4). The first saddle is forested and has a short side trail that leads to the top of a rocky knob.

After yet another steep upgrade and a couple of short switchbacks, the trail arrives at the second saddle at mile 0.5. A few steps off the trail onto a small rocky opening reveals an amazing panorama of the Three Sisters, Bachelor Butte, and Diamond Peak in the High Cascades, and also Fairview Peak and the Musick Guard Station.

If you can't go any farther, the middle saddle is a fine spot to relax and eat lunch, or at least take a long rest. The summit of Bohemia Mountain is well known among naturalists for its abundance and variety of butterflies.

Options: Should you choose to continue, a third saddle comes at mile 0.6, after an extremely steep upgrade and a couple more short, steep switchbacks.

Beyond the third saddle, the still-steep path makes its way around the main summit, then approaches the top over the rocks from the opposite direction. The final 200 feet to

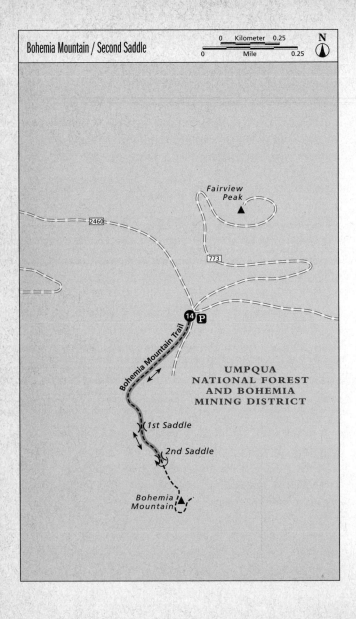

Bohemia Mountain / Second Saddle

0   Kilometer   0.25
0   Mile   0.25

N

Fairview Peak

2460

773

14 P

Bohemia Mountain Trail

UMPQUA
NATIONAL FOREST
AND BOHEMIA
MINING DISTRICT

1st Saddle

2nd Saddle

Bohemia
Mountain

the summit are an easy rock scramble. The summit itself, at mile 0.8, is a large, flat, cliff-top mesa that is 200 feet long and 20 feet wide. From there, on a clear day, you can see the entire chain of the Oregon High Cascades, including Mount Shasta (in California), Mount McLoughlin, the Crater Lake rim, Mount Thielsen, Diamond Peak, Mount Bachelor, the Three Sisters, Mount Jefferson, and Mount Hood (Oregon's highest peak, at 11,240 feet).

Miles and Directions

0.0 The second trailhead is located 200 feet up a side road from Bohemia Saddle. Begin hiking there, up a narrow, wooded ridge.

0.4 Arrive at the first saddle, which has a side trail to the top of a rock outcrop.

0.5 Arrive at the second saddle, a narrow, rocky gap just off the trail. This is the end of the "described" route and a possible turnaround spot.

(0.8) Arrive at the summit; turn around and return as you came.

1.0 to 1.6 (Depending on where you turned around.) Arrive back at the trailhead.

McKenzie River Area

15 McKenzie River Trail / Waterfalls Trail / Waterfalls Loop

This 3.0-mile loop visits the most scenic portion of the beautiful McKenzie River, through dense forest and past two of its most impressive highlights, the 70-foot Koosah Falls and the 100-foot Sahalie Falls. Beyond the falls area, the Waterfalls Trail ends at the junction with the 26-mile McKenzie River Trail. The route then crosses the river via a footbridge, and forms a loop by returning to the starting point via the other side of the river on a rougher path that offers a much different perspective on the two falls. The Waterfalls Trail and the McKenzie River Trail segment, taken together, constitute the "Waterfalls Loop."

Distance: 3.0-mile loop
Approximate hiking time: 1.5 hours
Difficulty: Easy
Elevation: 2,650 to 3,186 feet
Trail surface: Wide dirt tread with masonry stairways on the Waterfalls Trail (OR 126) side of the loop; much narrower, twisty, and quite rocky on the McKenzie River Trail (west) side.
Best season: Summer and fall. The trail may be wet or snowed over in winter and spring.
Other trail users: Use is heavy.

The McKenzie River Trail allows mountain bikes; the Waterfalls Trail does not.
Canine compatibility: Dogs must be leashed or under voice control.
Fees and permits: None
Schedule: Open 24 hours. OR 126 may be closed rarely and briefly due to snow in winter.
Maps: Willamette National Forest; USGS–Tamolitch Falls
Trail contacts: Willamette National Forest, 211 E. Seventh Ave., Federal Bldg., Eugene, OR 97440; (541) 465-6521;

www.fs.fed.us/r6/willamette/;   Willamette National Forest, Hwy.

and McKenzie Ranger District,   126, McKenzie Bridge, OR 97413

Finding the trailhead: From I-5, take the Springfield exit (#195-A), which is OR 126, the McKenzie River Highway (turn left past mile 9 to remain on 126). Continue to mile 55, past McKenzie Bridge, where OR 242 takes off on the right and OR 126 swings north. Stay on OR 126, but be advised that the milepost numbering on 126 changes at the 242 junction, from milepost 55 and ascending, to milepost 18 and descending. Near mile 6, turn left at the sign marked CARMEN DIVERSION RESERVOIR. The gravel side road goes past the dam and around the back of the lake to an auto bridge over the river, followed by a parking area and a vault toilet. Park in the parking area and walk back over the bridge to the trailhead on the left, immediately on the other (east) side. This is the beginning of the Waterfalls Trail and the Waterfalls Loop. The loop's far end (west) comes out by the vault toilet, where there is a short, connecting link to the McKenzie River Trail. GPS coordinates: N44 20.448, W122 00.162

The Hike

The McKenzie River National Recreation Trail is one of Oregon's great recreational gems. It begins near the town of McKenzie Bridge and runs for 26 miles to Clear Lake (source of the McKenzie), a couple miles up OR 126 from the Sahalie Falls turnoff. There are numerous intermediate trailheads along the 26-mile trail route.

For the least difficulty parking on the Waterfalls Loop, start the loop at the Carmen Reservoir. You may also begin at the Koosah Falls or Sahalie Falls parking areas (see Options below), but they tend to be far more crowded. Also, hiking counterclockwise puts you at the elaborate staircases in the uphill/upstream direction and offers a long downslope in the return direction.

Beginning at the trailhead located on the eastern end of the little auto bridge at Carmen Reservoir (the sign says WATERFALLS TRAIL), you are almost immediately in a dense Douglas-fir forest alongside the fast, beautiful, and rocky McKenzie River. After only 0.1 mile, you begin encountering connecting trails with log and masonry railings coming down from Icecap Springs Campground and the Koosah Falls parking area. When in doubt at the various trail junctions, always stay left (except for one short trail on the left that dead-ends at a little observation deck).

Koosah Falls comes into view at mile 0.3, and after several fancy masonry staircases, the path hits the top of the falls at mile 0.5. Koosah Falls is a straight plunge of about 70 feet, with a huge volume of water.

It's only 0.3 mile from Koosah Falls to Sahalie Falls, with Sahalie coming into view very soon after leaving the top of Koosah. Sahalie Falls is a popular spot, so there will be a lot of people there, along with several elaborate side trails down from the parking lot.

There is some disagreement about the height of Sahalie Falls, with figures ranging from 100 feet to 140 feet. The most reasonable figure gives the height of the actual falls at 100 feet and the immense cascade at the base (best seen from the other side of the river on the return loop) at another 40 feet. The 100-foot section is a vertical plunge over a wide, undercut rim, with a much narrower falls off to one side, tumbling over the same rim but separated from the main falls by a large chunk of lava.

Atop a lengthy staircase, the trail reaches a railed lookout deck at the top of Sahalie Falls (mile 0.8). Beyond this point, the trail becomes narrower and much less crowded as it winds along the river across a fairly level forested flat for

0.6 mile. At mile 1.5, the Waterfalls Trail ends and the path arrives at the junction with the McKenzie River Trail. Turn left and cross the narrow, single-log footbridge with railings.

The remainder of the route, on the McKenzie's west side, is much narrower and more twisty and rocky than the trail on the east side. Immediately over the footbridge, the path climbs to the top of a large bluff and then levels off as it approaches Sahalie Falls. The view of the top of the falls from this vantage point (mile 2.2) is outstanding—much better than the view from the lookout deck on the other side.

Look for a little wooden stile bridge near the beginning of the return trail that climbs up, over, and down the other side of an immense log. Usually, Forest Service personnel simply cut away a log when it falls across the trail; why they didn't in this case is unknown.

Beyond Sahalie, the path winds around among the rocks and drops down to Koosah again, at mile 2.5. At mile 2.9, you arrive at the little link trail (on the left) to the Carmen Reservoir parking lot, coming out near the vault toilet. Hike down the link trail, across the parking lot, and over the auto bridge, arriving back at the original trailhead at mile 3.0.

Options: If you're not interested in the entire loop, park at Carmen Reservoir and hike to the two falls and back in 1.6 miles, either on the Waterfalls Trail or the McKenzie River Trail. To visit just Koosah Falls, turn off OR 126 at Icecap Springs Campground, and then turn right for the Koosah Falls observation area. A short railed trail leads down to the falls and connects with the Waterfalls Trail. The turnoff for the Sahalie Falls observation area is located 0.5 mile on OR 126 from Icecap Springs. Again, a short

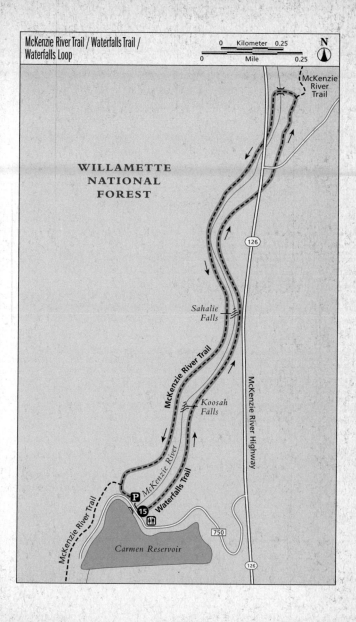

McKenzie River Trail / Waterfalls Trail /
Waterfalls Loop

0   Kilometer   0.25

0   Mile   0.25

N

McKenzie
River
Trail

WILLAMETTE
NATIONAL
FOREST

126

Sahalie
Falls

McKenzie River Trail

Koosah
Falls

McKenzie River Highway

McKenzie River

P

15

Waterfalls Trail

McKenzie River Trail

750

Carmen Reservoir

126

railed connecting trail leads down to the Waterfalls Trail. You may also hike from one observation area to the other and back in about a mile.

Miles and Directions

0.0 Park at Carmen Reservoir and walk to the Waterfalls Trail trailhead on the east end of the auto bridge.

0.5 Pass and climb Koosah Falls.

0.8 Pass and climb Sahalie Falls.

1.5 Arrive at the junction with McKenzie River Trail, which marks the end of the Waterfalls Trail. Turn left and cross the footbridge.

2.2 Excellent view of Sahalie Falls from the other side of the river.

2.5 Pass Koosah Falls on the other side of the river.

2.9 Arrive at the short link trail back to the Carmen Reservoir parking area. Turn left.

3.0 Complete the loop.

16 McKenzie River Trail / Blue Pool

This is the very definition of an "easy" and "best" hike. The route, a portion of the 26-mile McKenzie River National Recreation Trail, takes you on a 4.0-mile (out and back) walk along the beautiful McKenzie River, through an enchanted old-growth forest, then up onto lava flows and cliffs above the river, and finally, to an incredible, intensely blue pool at the base of a dry waterfall (Tamolitch Falls). For 2.0 miles above the falls (outside the described hike), the riverbed is completely dry most of the year, as the water runs underground, with the river fully and spectacularly re-emerging at Blue Pool.

Distance: 4.0 miles out and back
Approximate hiking time: 2 hours (round-trip)
Difficulty: Easy
Elevation: 2,200 to 2,500 feet
Trail surface: Dirt; the second mile is much twistier and rockier than the first mile.
Best season: At an elevation of 2,500 feet, there may or may not be snow in winter, but the trail will be muddy and the water high. In summer, the route is cooled by the dense forest canopy.
Other trail users: This is considered one of the ten best mountain bike paths in the US. Hiker and biker use is heavy.
Canine compatibility: Dogs must be leashed or under voice control.
Fees and permits: None
Schedule: Open 24 hours. OR 126 may be closed rarely and briefly due to snow in winter.
Maps: Willamette National Forest; USGS–Tamolitch Lake
Trail contacts: Willamette National Forest, 211 E. Seventh Ave., Federal Bldg., Eugene, OR 97440; (541) 465-6521; www.fs.fed.us/r6/willamette/; and McKenzie Ranger District, Willamette National Forest, Hwy. 126, McKenzie Bridge, OR 97413

Finding the trailhead: From I-5, take the Springfield exit (#195-A), which is OR 126, the McKenzie River Highway. Continue for 55 miles (turning left past mile 9 to remain on 126), past the town of McKenzie Bridge, to where OR 242 takes off on the right and OR 126 swings north. Stay on OR 126, but be advised that the milepost numbering on 126 changes at the 242 junction, from milepost 55 and ascending, to milepost 18 and descending. Near mile 12, turn left where the sign says TRAIL BRIDGE RESERVOIR. Follow the side road past the dam and power plant to a sign marked BLUE POOL TRAILHEAD ½ MILE. Continue on the pavement and gravel to the trailhead and follow the path to the right. GPS coordinates: N44 17.406, W122 02.127

The Hike

This route, along a 2.0-mile segment of the McKenzie River National Recreation Trail, may be the best hike in this entire book. For the first mile, the path is wide, easy, and level, crossing two wooden footbridges over side creeks. The route mostly runs at the level of the nearby river, which is fast, rocky, and amazingly scenic. The surrounding forest, with an overstory consisting of the "big three" of the Pacific Northwest—immense old Douglas-fir, western redcedar, and western hemlock—is spooky and enchanting, especially the wide-based redcedars. Also found in abundance are dwarf Oregongrape, trillium, sword fern, whortleberry, Douglas maple, and bigleaf maple.

During the first mile, hikers might feel like they could easily run into leprechauns or an Ewok village. The area verges on being a temperate rain forest, so look for "nurse trees"—old, rotted logs with trees (usually hemlocks) growing out of them.

Toward the end of mile 1.0, the path starts winding around and through lava flows, gradually climbing to about

50 feet above the river, with many sheer cliffs and over-looks. This portion of the route is slower and a little more difficult than the initial portion, with numerous short up and down pitches. The forest thins out a bit here, and the trees are considerably smaller.

Look for "ropy" lava as you walk. There's not much of it, but the wavy or ropy surface of these interesting rocks (technically called *pahoehoe* lava) indicates that when the lava melted, it was rapidly flowing and swirling. Notice also the bubbles in the rock (called vesicles), caused by gas escaping as the lava hardened.

Precisely at mile 2.0, you will arrive at a fantastic over-look of Tamolitch Falls (dropping about 35 feet) and Blue Pool. The pool covers about three acres in the bottom of a horseshoe-shaped, steep-sided basin, and is intensely blue due to its clarity, much like Crater Lake. The elegant, droopy-branched trees on the far side of the pool are west-ern hemlock.

Unless you visit during a very wet winter, Tamolitch Falls, at the upper end of the basin, will be dry. And, in fact, the riverbed on the trail continuing northward will be dry for the next 2.0 miles upstream, to Carmen Diversion Res-ervoir. The reservoir diverts all the McKenzie's surface water to nearby Smith Reservoir. However, at the diversion point, the majority of the McKenzie's water disappears underground anyhow, possibly into lava tubes that underlie much of the area. (You can observe collapsed lava tubes along the trail.) The river fully reemerges again at Blue Pool.

It's another 0.1 mile from the observation area to the upper end of the pool basin, atop a high cliff. From there, you can scramble down to the top of the falls.

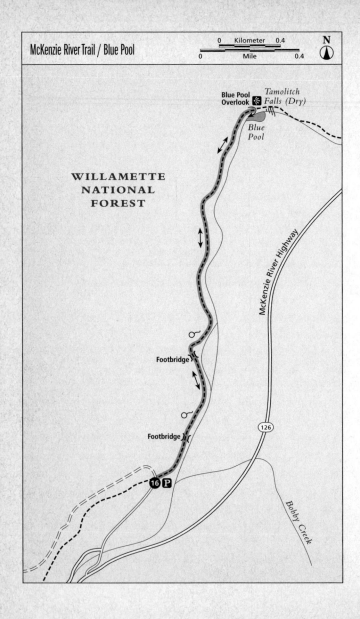

McKenzie River Trail / Blue Pool

0 Kilometer 0.4

0 Mile 0.4

N

Blue Pool
Overlook

*Tamolitch
Falls (Dry)*

Blue
Pool

WILLAMETTE
NATIONAL
FOREST

McKenzie River Highway

Footbridge

Footbridge

126

16 P

Bobby Creek

Options: From both the trailhead south and Blue Pool north, the McKenzie River Trail continues on. The total length is 26 miles.

Miles and Directions

0.0 Park at the trailhead area and start walking on the trail to the right.

2.0 Arrive at the Blue Pool overlook. Either continue on or turn around and return to the trailhead. There are other observation points a little farther up the trail, and there is a spot where you can climb down to the top of the dry Tamolitch Falls.

4.0 Arrive back at the trailhead.

17 Linton Lake (Three Sisters Wilderness)

This easy to moderate trail visits a beautiful, fishable, eighty-acre lake dammed by a large lava flow and surrounded on three sides by steep, forested slopes. Hikers can catch glimpses of Linton Falls, at the far end of the lake, in an area inaccessible by trail. By some measurements, Linton Falls is 615 feet high, making it nearly as high as Multnomah Falls, Oregon's highest.

Distance: 3.4 miles out and back

Approximate hiking time: 2 hours (round-trip)

Difficulty: Easy to moderate

Elevation: 3,502 to 3,650 feet

Trail surface: Narrow dirt; rocky in places

Best season: Spring, summer, and fall (OR 242 is closed in winter; the trail and lake are usually snow-free by mid-May or early June)

Other trail users: Hikers only; use is moderate to heavy.

Canine compatibility: Dogs must be leashed or under voice control.

Fees and permits: National forest parking fee

Schedule: Open 24 hours in season. OR 242 is closed in winter.

Maps: Willamette National Forest; USGS–Linton Lake

Trail contacts: Willamette National Forest, 211 E. Seventh Ave., Federal Bldg., Eugene, OR 97440; (541) 465-6521; www.fs.fed.us/r6/willamette/; and McKenzie Ranger District, Willamette National Forest, Hwy. 126, McKenzie Bridge, OR 97413

Finding the trailhead: From I-5, take the Springfield exit (#195-A), which is OR 126, the McKenzie River Highway. Turn left past mile 9 to remain on OR 126. Continue past the town of McKenzie Bridge and milepost 55 to where OR 242 takes off on the right 126 swings north. Turn onto OR 242 for about 9 miles. Eleven miles up, near mile 66, at Alder Springs Campground, there is a well-marked (and often-crowded) parking area for the Linton Lake trailhead. GPS coordinates: N44 10.617, W121 54.828

The Hike

From the wooden steps at the trailhead across the highway from the campground, follow the path through a fairly young and open forest of Douglas-fir, western white pine, western hemlock, and western redcedar, with rhododendron and Douglas maple in the understory. The path is mostly level for the first 0.5 mile. At mile 0.6 it begins climbing, and at mile 0.7 it meets a side trail (see Options below). Take a hard right at the junction with the side trail.

Past the junction, the path makes its way across and over several large lava flows and rubble slopes, with steep but fairly short upgrades and downgrades. At mile 1.2, the trail arrives at the lake, high above the outlet creek (there's a side trail down to the lake here; see Options). The next 0.5 mile, until the path dead-ends, contours high above the lake in a slight downward trend, with occasional steep side paths down to the shore. There are no really good views of the lake from the main trail because of the dense forest. However, look for glimpses of the top 100 feet or so of Linton Falls here, high up the ridge on the other side of the lake.

The trail dead-ends at mile 1.7 at Obsidian Creek, where there is a large campsite. The lakeshore here is quite brushy, and again, views of the lake are not good. The lake covers eighty acres, and unlike other mountain lakes in the

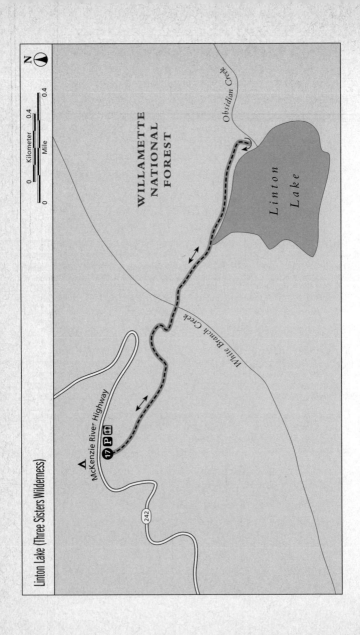

Linton Lake (Three Sisters Wilderness)

vicinity, was formed by a lava dam rather than a defunct ice age glacier.

Linton Falls is a series of plunges, terraces, and steep cascades at the far end of the lake, with a combined 615-foot drop. The highest single plunge is 150 feet. The total combined height of upper and lower Multnomah Falls, including the intermediate cascades, is 620 feet. With its highest single plunge of 545 feet, Multnomah Falls is considered the highest waterfall in the United States, outside of California's Yosemite Valley.

Unfortunately, Linton Falls is inaccessible, and it is not possible to see the entire falls from any vantage point. Salt Creek Falls, at 284 feet, rather than Linton Falls, is usually listed as Oregon's second-highest waterfall after Multnomah Falls.

Options: Although there is no actual trail around the lake, people walk around it frequently, and shoreside vistas are splendid.

The best view of Linton Falls is from the shore near the beginning of the lake's main outlet creek. The main trail passes a very steep and infrequently maintained side trail down to the outlet (the side trail may be blocked by fallen logs but you should be able to find a way around them). This short but difficult side route is highly recommended. Once at the bottom, follow the path across the green meadow to the top of the lava outcrop, where you can see perhaps 200 feet of Linton Falls.

It is also possible to hike off-trail around the lakeshore and up Linton Creek to see the bottom 85 feet of the falls.

The side trail at mile 0.7 is a shortcut from OR 242. To find the shortcut trailhead, drive 0.5 mile past the main trailhead at Alder Springs Campground, to a sharp switchback. A couple of wide spots on the shoulder just before the switchback accommodate two or three cars each. The unmarked trailhead is located just before the guardrail at the switchback. The side trail is extremely steep and 0.2 mile long, so it saves about 0.5 mile—but then you have to hike back up it.

Miles and Directions

0.0 Park and begin hiking at the little stairway at the trailhead.

0.7 Pass the junction with the side trail (take a sharp right). This is the beginning of the lava flows where the path has a few steep spots.

1.2 Arrive at the lake outlet and the side trail down to the lake.

1.7 The main trail ends at the Obsidian Creek campsite. This is the turnaround.

3.4 Arrive back at the trailhead.

18 Proxy Falls Loop (Three Sisters Wilderness)

This short, easy loop visits two spectacular waterfalls in the Cascade Mountains, each about 200 feet high.

Distance: 1.6-mile loop (includes distance along OR 242, between the two trailheads)

Approximate hiking time: 45 minutes

Difficulty: Easy

Elevation: 3,250 feet

Trail surface: Dirt

Best season: OR 242 is closed in winter; the trail is usually snow-free by late May or mid-June.

Other trail users: Hikers only; use is heavy.

Canine compatibility: Dogs must be leashed or under voice control.

Fees and permits: National forest parking fee

Schedule: Open 24 hours in season. OR 242 is closed in winter.

Maps: Willamette National Forest; USGS–Linton Lake

Trail contacts: Willamette National Forest, 211 E. Seventh Ave., Federal Bldg., Eugene, OR 97440; (541) 465-6521; www .fs.fed.us/r6/willamette/; and McKenzie Ranger District, Willamette National Forest, Hwy. 126, McKenzie Bridge, OR 97413

Finding the trailhead: From I-5, take the Springfield exit (#195-A), which is OR 126, the McKenzie River Highway. Turn left past mile 9 to remain on OR 126. Continue past the town of McKenzie Bridge and milepost 55, to where OR 242 takes off on the right and 126 swings north. Turn onto OR 242 for about 9 miles. Near milepost 64, there is a well-marked (and often-crowded) parking area for the Proxy Falls trailhead. GPS coordinates: N44 10.076, W121 55.630

The Hike

The sign at the trailhead advises users to begin the loop using the trailhead on the right, not the left, and then to proceed counterclockwise. However, if you start on the left, as most people seem to do, it is only one-third as far to the first falls turnoff.

Both the trailhead map and the Forest Service detail map incorrectly show the right- and left-hand loops as about the same length. Actually, the left-hand side of the loop is much shorter. The right-hand loop, although longer, is still pretty short, quite scenic, and highly recommended, crossing some interesting and rugged lava outcrops. The right-hand loop is also a little steeper.

Beginning on the right, as suggested by the trailhead sign, the path follows the highway for about 200 feet, makes its way over the lava outcrops, and then winds through the woods until reaching the first falls turnoff. You may find yourself wondering, as you hike, how a 200-foot waterfall could possibly fit into this scene.

At mile 0.7, you arrive at the junction with the Lower Proxy Falls side trail, taking off on the right. Signs there indicate the loop trail and the direction to the trailhead, but not Lower Proxy Falls. It is 0.1 mile up the side trail to the falls overlook, and another 0.1 mile to the base of the falls. Lower Proxy Falls is an immense vertical drop hugging a steep rock face that splits the flow in two. It is indeed one of the better waterfalls you'll find, and as to its location, it falls down the very lava flow you've been walking over.

Back on the main loop, hike for another 0.2 mile to a second side trail, also taking off on the right. Again, signs there indicate the loop trail and the direction to the

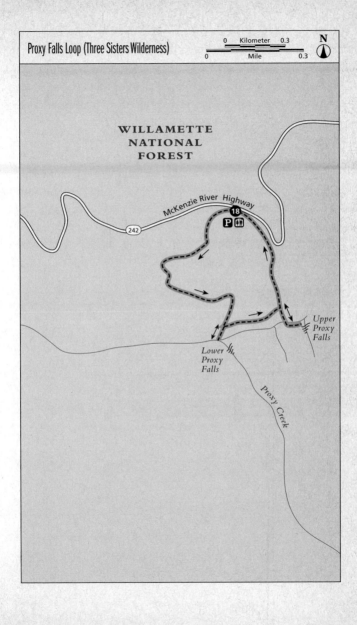

trailhead, but not Upper Proxy Falls. After 0.1 mile on the side trail, you reach the Upper Falls (which are not on the same creek as the lower falls). They are the same height as the Lower Falls, but not as steep, tumbling down a series of steep rock faces and terraces. Interestingly, the fairly large collecting pool at the base has no outlet. Since the entire area is a lava flow, the water either disappears into hollow subterranean lava tubes, which are quite common in the Cascade Mountains, or into the soil-filled seams between bedded lava layers, where the water can wash out the soil and form an underground river. This is all very theoretical.

Back at the junction, another 0.3 mile will complete the loop back to the trailhead, over lava outcrops that are not nearly as extensive or rugged as the loop's initial leg.

Miles and Directions

0.0 Start hiking from the trailhead on the right.

0.7 Arrive at the junction with Lower Proxy Falls Trail; turn right.

0.8 Arrive at the Lower Proxy Falls overlook. The side trail takes you to the base of the falls in another 0.1 mile.

0.9 Back at the junction with the main trail; turn right.

1.1 Arrive at the junction with Upper Proxy Falls Trail; turn right.

1.2 The side trail ends at the base of Upper Proxy Falls.

1.3 Back at the main trail; turn right.

1.6 Complete the loop and return to the trailhead sign and parking area.

Oakridge / Willamette Pass

19 Salt Creek Falls

Salt Creek Falls, at 284 feet high, is second in Oregon only to Multnomah Falls, and this short hike (0.4 mile one–way) is absolutely spectacular. A final 0.1 mile beyond the "official" hike is far too steep for inclusion, but you are welcome to try it. In 0.4 mile, the trail takes you from the parking lot to the cliff edge, 50 feet above the top of Salt Creek Falls, then down to an observation deck 100 feet above the bottom of the falls. The final 0.1 mile descends to the edge of the collecting pool at the base of the falls.

Distance: 0.8 mile out and back to the lower viewing platform; 1.0 mile out and back to base of falls

Approximate hiking time: 30 minutes (round-trip)

Difficulty: Described hike is easy to moderate, but the final, optional 0.1 mile is more challenging.

Elevation: 4,185 feet (trail high point); 3,950 feet (lower observation deck); 3,850 feet (base of falls)

Trail surface: Paved, then dirt

Best season: Summer and fall. The access road is plowed year-round, and while it's beautiful in winter, the trail is rarely snow-free. The final 0.1 mile to the

bottom can be treacherous in wet weather.

Other trail users: Hikers only; very heavy use

Canine compatibility: Dogs must be leashed or under voice control.

Fees and permits: Parking permit available on-site

Schedule: Open 24 hours. OR 58 and the access road experience heavy snowfall in winter, but are kept open except for occasional brief closures.

Maps: Willamette National Forest; USGS–Willamette Pass/Diamond Peak

Trail contact: Oakridge Ranger District, Willamette National Forest, 46375 Hwy. 58, Westfir, OR 97492; (541) 782-2291

Finding the trailhead: From I-5, get off at exit 188-A and take OR 58 toward Oakridge, Willamette Pass, and Klamath Falls. Oakridge is at mile 35, and the Salt Creek Falls turnoff is at mile 57, on the right. At the turnoff, continue on the access road for about 1 mile to the parking loop, trailhead, and restrooms. Parking for the Diamond Creek Falls Loop Trail is a little farther down the access loop. GPS coordinates: N43 36.725, W122 07.643

The Hike

At the parking area, there are plumbed restrooms and an informational display. For the trail to the bottom, follow the paved path to the right of the informational display for 200 feet to the falls overlook, which is paved and has concrete and metal railings. The railed overlook extends for about 300 feet along the cliff top, offering excellent views of the waterfall's 284-foot plunge over a 350-foot cliff of undercut basaltic lava. Salt Creek is more a small river than a creek, so there is usually quite a lot of water tumbling over the precipice.

Heading to the right at the overlook area, the paved/railed portion climbs a stairway, with the actual dirt trail starting at the top, where the developed area ends. The dirt trail almost touches OR 58, and then makes its way through a beautiful Douglas-fir forest, with the falls always in view. The path is wide and protected by a log railing as it drops steeply downhill, in a series of switchbacks, to the lower observation deck.

At the lower observation deck, which is made of logs, 0.4 mile from the trailhead, the manicured trail ends, as does the "official" route.

Options: From the lower observation deck, the entire 0.1 mile of remaining trail can be seen. Note that "0.1

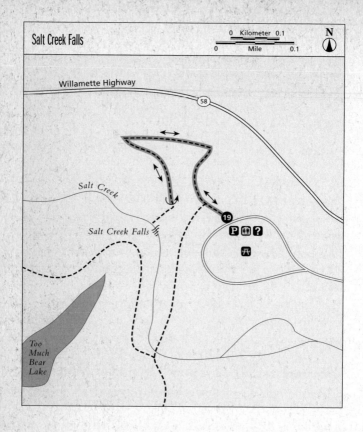

Salt Creek Falls

Willamette Highway

58

Salt Creek

Salt Creek Falls

19

Too
Much
Bear
Lake

0   Kilometer 0.1

0   Mile   0.1

N

mile" refers to horizontal map distance. Since this segment is extremely steep, the true distance is longer than 0.1 mile.

The last segment shoots straight downhill for 75 feet or so, over loose dirt and rocks. It then makes three tight switchbacks down an immense, rocky talus slope before hitting the final loose and slippery, straight-downhill pitch.

This final portion is well worth the effort (even though you must also climb back up it). The base of Salt Creek Falls is one of the most awesome and enchanting places you're likely to find. The gray-black 350-foot-high cliff, covered with yellow-green moss, is breathtaking, as are the surges of falling water that constantly change shape.

Even if you don't hike the final segment, just looking at it makes the hike back up to the upper observation area seem much easier by contrast.

The Diamond Creek Falls Loop Trail begins a little farther down the access loop road, in its own parking area just beyond the Salt Creek Falls parking area. This 2.5-mile loop trail visits the 80-foot-high, fan-shaped falls in 1.0 mile (with a side trail to the top). It then passes Lower Diamond Creek Falls and, at mile 1.5, Too Much Bear Lake. The final mile returns to the Salt Creek Falls area along the cliff top. The loop is wheelchair-accessible to Diamond Creek Falls.

Miles and Directions

0.0 Park and start hiking to the right of the trailhead kiosk. Continue 200 feet to the upper observation area. Thus far, the route is paved.

0.1 Head to the right, along the rim and railing, to the top of the stairs where the dirt trail begins. Follow the dirt trail.

0.4 Arrive at the lower observation deck. This is the turnaround for the described hike.

(0.5) The trail ends at the base of the falls.

0.8 Arrive back at the trailhead.

20 Erma Bell Lakes
(Three Sisters Wilderness)

This easy, charming trail leads to two beautiful alpine lakes in the Three Sisters Wilderness, with a thundering 40-foot waterfall in between. The path to the lower lake is nearly level and is considered wheelchair-accessible.

Distance: 4.6 miles out and back

Approximate hiking time: 2 hours (round-trip)

Difficulty: Easy to moderate

Elevation: 4,450 to 4,600 feet

Trail surface: Wide and covered with conifer needles; very few rocks

Best season: Mid-June to mid-Nov

Other trail users: Moderate use; hikers only

Canine compatibility: Dogs must be leashed or under voice control.

Fees and permits: Pay either a parking fee, or a fee for using the walk-in campground at the trailhead.

Schedule: Open 24 hours in season. FR 19 may experience winter closures. FR 1957 is impassable due to snow from late fall to late spring.

Maps: Willamette National Forest; USGS–Waldo Mountain

Trail contact: Oakridge Ranger District, Willamette National Forest, 46375 Hwy. 58, Westfir, OR 97492; (541) 782-2291

Finding the trailhead: From I-5 at exit 188-A, take the Willamette River Highway (OR 58) east for 31 miles to the Middle Fork Ranger Station. Opposite the ranger station, turn left onto Westfir Road (following signs to the Huckleberry Flat OHV Trail) and proceed for 1.0 mile. At the "T" junction just across the bridge, turn left and continue for another mile to the town of Westfir. At the covered bridge (the longest in Oregon), FR 19 takes off (this is the Aufderheide Scenic Byway). Proceed 32 miles on the paved road to just before the Box Canyon Guard Station, where you will turn right (onto FR 1957), following signs to Skookum Creek Campground. Four miles up the gravel side road, park at the campground and follow the Erma Bell Lakes Trail past the wilderness boundary sign and over the little footbridge and creek. GPS coordinates: N43 51.707, W122 02.713

The Hike

The best of all hiking trails—when it comes to scenery and relaxation—are mountain pathways in the wilderness that wind through dense forest and emerge at exquisite and isolated alpine lakes. The Erma Bell Lakes Trail not only accomplishes all of that, but the trail is also virtually level for the first 1.7 miles—so level that it is considered wheelchair-accessible.

The path begins at Skookum Creek Campground at a trailhead sign and footbridge. The next 1.3 miles are absolutely level, and, although exquisitely beautiful, may be a little monotonous for some. You are in the understory of a dense, unbroken Douglas-fir forest, and all you can see are tree trunks and ground-level bunchberry dogwood and trillium plants. (Be prepared for lots of mosquitoes from the trail opening in mid-June to about mid-August.)

At mile 0.7, the route passes the junction with the Irish Mountain Trail, which you can follow to Otter Lake in about 0.7 mile (see Options below).

At mile 1.3, the trail gently bends to the left and begins a long, very easy downgrade to a creek crossing and footbridge (mile 1.5).

A short side trail at mile 1.7 leads to twenty-five-acre Lower Erma Bell Lake, a round, clear pool with rocky boulder slopes on three sides that rise up about 50 feet at the lake's far end. There are several excellent campsites nearby, and you can hear the upcoming waterfall everywhere in the lake basin.

Back on the trail, the path quickly dips down to another small footbridge over a creek with a small waterfall (mile 1.8). It then makes its way around the lake, climbing at a moderate grade to the top of the highest slope on the lakeshore. From the side trail at mile 1.7 to the waterfall at mile 2.2, the lower lake is always in view.

A short side trail leads to Erma Bell Falls, a massive and spectacular 40-foot plunge over a cliff. Back on the main trail, Upper Erma Bell Lake (twenty-eight acres) comes into view soon after, at mile 2.3.

Options: It's 0.7 mile (moderately steep) on the Irish Mountain Trail to Otter Lake, which is a little smaller than Lower Erma Bell Lake, but otherwise similar. The entire Erma Bell Lakes Trail is 5.0 miles long. It passes tiny Upper Erma Bell Lake at mile 3.0, Mud Lake at mile 4.0, and the turnoff to Williams Lake at mile 4.5, before finally emerging at the end of FR 514.

Miles and Directions

0.0 Park at the Skookum Creek Campground and look for a trailhead sign and footbridge off to the right.

0.7 Arrive at the junction with the Irish Mountain Trail, on the left. Go straight.

1.5 The trail crosses a small creek via a footbridge.

1.7 Arrive at the short side trail, on the left, leading to Lower Erma Bell Lake.

1.8 Back on the main trail, pass the lower lake's outlet creek and a small waterfall.

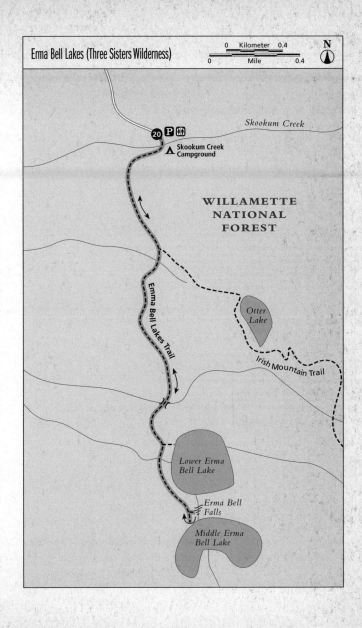

Erma Bell Lakes (Three Sisters Wilderness)

0   Kilometer   0.4
0   Mile   0.4

N

Skookum Creek

20 P 🚻
▲ Skookum Creek
Campground

WILLAMETTE
NATIONAL
FOREST

Emma Bell Lakes Trail

Otter
Lake

Irish Mountain Trail

Lower Erma
Bell Lake

Erma Bell
Falls

Middle Erma
Bell Lake

2.2 Look for an unmarked 100-foot side trail on the left that leads to Erma Bell Falls.

2.3 Back on the main trail, you will arrive at Middle Erma Bell Lake. This is the turnaround for the described hike.

4.6 Arrive back at the trailhead.

About the Authors

Art Bernstein is the author of thirteen nature and hiking guides, including Falcon's *Hiking Oregon's Southern Cascades and Siskiyous* and *Weird Hikes*. He has an MS in Forestry from the University of Michigan, is an avid hiker and naturalist, and has lived in Grants Pass, Oregon, since 1972.

Lynn Bernstein is the official photographer, record keeper, GPS tracker, and motivator—and the person who makes it all fun. She has lived in Oregon since 2003 and loves it!

WHAT'S SO SPECIAL ABOUT UNSPOILED, NATURAL PLACES?

Beauty   Solitude   Wildness   Freedom   Quiet   Adventure
Serenity   Inspiration   Wonder   Excitement
Relaxation   Challenge

There's a lot to love about our treasured public lands, and the reasons are different for each of us. Whatever your reasons are, the national **Leave No Trace** education program will help you discover special outdoor places, enjoy them, and preserve them—today and for those who follow. By practicing and passing along these simple principles, you can help protect the special places you love from being loved to death.

THE PRINCIPLES OF **LEAVE NO TRACE**

- Plan ahead and prepare
- Travel and camp on durable surfaces
- Dispose of waste properly
- Leave what you find
- Minimize campfire impacts
- Respect wildlife
- Be considerate of other visitors

Leave No Trace is a national nonprofit organization dedicated to teaching responsible outdoor recreation skills and ethics to everyone who enjoys spending time outdoors.

To learn more or to become a member, please visit us at www.LNT.org or call (800) 332-4100.

Leave No Trace, P.O. Box 997, Boulder, CO 80306